With the collaboration of Valeria Ferraretto

Acknowledgments

We want to thank:

Richard Appelbaum, Professor Emeritus, Global Studies, UCSB.

Aashish Mehta, Associate Professor, Global Studies, UCSB.

Agnieszka Elzbieta Stawinoga, PhD, Senior Researcher, Eurac Research Bolzano/Bozen.

Daniela Pichler, former intern, Eurac Research Bolzano/Bozen.

Pavel Raus, former intern, Eurac Research Bolzano/Bozen.

Simone Sartor, former intern, Eurac Research Bolzano/Bozen.

Contents

About the Authors

Ingrid Kofler is senior researcher at the Center for Advanced Studies at Eurac Research Bozen-Bolzano, Italy. She holds a PhD in sociology from the University of Paris Descartes-Sorbonne and the University of Roma Tre. She was visiting researcher at the University of California, Santa Barbara, and at the Hamburgisches Weltwirtschaftsinstitut (HWWI).

Elisa Innerhofer is senior researcher at the Center for Advanced Studies at Eurac Research Bozen-Bolzano, Italy. She studied international economics, business science and political science at the University of Innsbruck and the Marquette University in Milwaukee (WI, USA) and holds a PhD in economics from the Catholic University of Eichstaett-Ingolstadt in Germany.

Anja Marcher, MA is a researcher at the Center for Advanced Studies at Eurac Research Bozen-Bolzano, Italy, and junior fellow at the Institute for Advanced Studies (IHS) in Vienna. She holds a Master of Arts in human geography from the University of Vienna and is PhD student in geography at the Catholic University of Eichstätt-Ingolstadt in Germany.

Mirjam Gruber, MA is a researcher at the Center for Advanced Studies of Eurac Research Bozen-Bolzano, Italy. She did her master's degree in political science (major) and sustainable development (minor) at the University of Bern, Switzerland, and is PhD student in political science at the University of Leipzig in Germany.

Harald Pechlaner is head of the Center for Advanced Studies at Eurac Research Bozen-Bolzano, Italy, and Professor of Tourism and head of the Center for Entrepreneurship at the Catholic University of Eichstätt-Ingolstadt, Germany.

Valeria Ferraretto, MA is junior researcher at the Center for Advanced Studies of Eurac Research Bozen-Bolzano, Italy. She holds a master's degree in European and international studies from the University of Trento, Italy.

List of Figures

List of Tables

1

Introduction

Abstract This chapter serves as an introduction to the topic of this book, that is the future of high-skilled workers and related regional problems and global challenges in a rapidly changing world. In this chapter, we introduce the main definition and the structure of the book, as well as the methods used in our research.

Keywords High-skilled • Future of work • Methods

The shortage of a (highly) skilled workforce in many sectors, the increasing aging of the population, rapid technological changes and digitalization are transforming the nature of work. Technological change due to increasing digitalization, increasing complexity due to the affluence of information, changed customer behavior due to rising expectations, high competitive intensity due to disruption, declining productivity due to excessive bureaucracy, a threat to performance due to a lack of skilled workers, more individualization due to increased self-confidence—these are just a few examples of drivers transforming the world of work. These

I. Kofler et al., *The Future of High-Skilled Workers*,
https://doi.org/10.1007/978-3-030-42871-6_1

shifts are challenging the whole labor market. Enterprises, organizations, workers, regional and national labor markets are in a global competition for (highly) qualified and specialized workers.

For some years now, the lack of (highly) qualified personnel has dominated newspapers: companies complain about lost revenues, want to increase their number of employees or have recruiting problems. It is now a generalized opinion that location and production factors are crucial for workers. The attractiveness of cities, regions or countries is an important driver but is creating inequalities at the regional, individual and global levels as well as between urban and rural areas. The flexibility of an internationally mobile workforce and the increasing speed at which skill requirements are changing produce disparities at the spatial, social and economic levels. Workers are also under pressure to perform and adapt to the requirements of the market and are often over- or underqualified.

Changes in the future of work are affecting both developed and less-developed economies. One of the biggest concerns is related to "talents" or "high-skilled workers." There is no common definition of who these talents are, but in general, these people seem to be the central actors of future economies and the future of work, as their innovation and creativity are considered the key drivers for economic development and growth. Companies, regions and nations are in a global competition for these talents. It seems that a high proportion of these highly qualified and highly creative people make a significant contribution not only to economic growth but also to the competitiveness and innovative ability of a location. The global competition for the best is continuously increasing, particularly in specific sectors. If a certain job, company, region or country is not attractive, many qualified workers can opt for more attractive alternative offers elsewhere, creating disparities between regions. This flexibility of an internationally mobile, highly skilled workforce and rapidly changing skill requirements challenge "competing" countries and companies to continuously rethink and adapt their strategies and offers in order to increase their ability to attract and retain highly skilled workers.

In 1998, Mc. Kinsey & Company launched the so-called war for talent publishing a report concluding that the most important resource of the future would be globally dynamic and flexible "talents" with technological literacy. The whole discourse following Mellander's and Florida's (2011, 2012) concept of "the rise of talents" made companies, regions and governments aware of the need to gather talents, but inequalities are widening because of the creation of a new elite of talents, who tend to cluster together (for instance, in urban areas). Moreover, the balance of power has shifted from the companies to workers (Economist, 2006). Global demographic and economic trends along with greater mobility, the brain drain and a knowledge-driven transformation of enterprises are factors causing the battle of talents. Additionally, diversity in terms of culture, gender and working generation is increasing, causing a new order of work (Beechler & Woodward, 2009). The most competitive economies and enterprises will be those attracting talent in a global labor market and these international exchanges will need governments to invest in education and human capital (Douglass & Edelstein, 2009).

However, the driving forces and processes behind this race to attract talents are global trends and megatrends shaping the future. For this reason, in order to understand changing labor markets, global processes and developments should be taken into consideration from an interdisciplinary perspective. What ongoing developments are influencing the future of work for highly skilled workers? What are the social, economic and political implications of these developments? Who are the talents of tomorrow? Which regions or cities are the most attractive? What does that mean on a global level and at a more regional level for Europe? In order to answer these questions, our book offers insights from an interdisciplinary research project carried out with the aim of bringing together regional problems and global challenges using a mixed-method approach.

1.1 Definitions and Structure of the Book

The term "talent" has many different meanings in the literature. Some definitions are based on the educational level, others on skills and many more combine different qualifications and abilities. For instance, according to McKinsey talent refers to "the best and the brightest" and it is "the sum of a person's abilities, his or her intrinsic gifts, skills, knowledge, experience, intelligence, judgment, attitude, character, and drives. It also includes his or her ability to learn and grow" (Michaels, Handfield-Jones, & Axelrod, 2001, p. xii). In this definition, the level of education does not play an explicit role, whereas Florida describes talent as the creative class, creative professionals and "individuals with high human capital, measured as the percentage of the population with a bachelor's degree and above" (2002, p. 1). On the individual level, talents could be people who "regularly demonstrate exceptional ability–and achievement" (Williams, 2000, p. 35) and thus make an essential contribution to ensure the competitiveness and thus the future of a company. There are many other similar approaches, and in brief, it can be asserted that the so-called talents possess specific knowledge and qualifications, together with social and methodological competences and skills. Thus, talents can be very diverse, and in this book, we use the terms highly skilled, high-skilled, highly qualified and high-qualified as synonyms for talents.

Part I of the book (Chaps. 2, 3, 4 and 5) will give an overview of the main trends shaping the future of work, while Part II (Chaps. 6 and 7) will focus on Europe and its regions. Both parts of the book are enriched by insights and statements from interviews with experts, a Delphi study and other results from research in the year 2018. Chapter 2 focuses on two main megatrends shaping the future of work—technology and demographic change—and shows how new technologies and, in particular, digitization will introduce new tasks and new ways of thinking to the world of work. The aging and shrinking of industrialized societies as along with migration and feminization are also important elements changing the future of work. Chapter 3 illustrates how growing skills shortages are generating political and socio-economic tension. Even though research shows that there are different levels of skills mismatch, the knowledge economy pressures toward an "academicization" of society, with different implications in terms of social inequalities. Chapter 4 focuses on the challenges that high-skilled workers will face in terms of organization of work and life and how a work-life balance is key for them. Their focus is not only on how well jobs are paid but also on the flexibility and democracy of organizations. Chapter 5 shows the importance of location factors and which factors are important for regions and nations to retain and attract the highly skilled, also showing disparities between urban and rural areas. Chapter 6 introduces Part II of the book where we change from a global to a more regional perspective. Moreover, this section presents the European Region's Talents Competitiveness Index, comparing 282 regions of Europe. Finally, Chap. 7 illustrates the challenges regions are facing in this global competition for talents by focusing on the specific case study of the region South Tyrol, located in the middle of the Alps.

Since rapid changes are radically altering our daily life, individuals have a growing sense of disconnectedness and uncertainty. This makes the future more malleable than ever and therefore it is even more important to understand the complexity of the world. The dynamics and complexity of the future labor market for the highly skilled cannot be captured adequately within the framework of any single academic discipline. They can only be understood combining insights from fields including economics, politics, political economy, sociology, geography, organizational theories, development studies, international relations, ICT and gender studies.

1.2 Methods

This book provides an interdisciplinary overview of the phenomenon using various theoretical approaches from different disciplines, bringing together sociology, economy and management, geography, political science and international relations. Complex issues like the future of work question traditional disciplinary boundaries and require cross- and interdisciplinary thinking. Interdisciplinarity is more than analyzing the phenomenon from different disciplinary views and putting them together. Interdisciplinarity requires finding answers between and beyond the disciplines, going beyond disciplinary boundaries having a holistic claim, whether in the recognition of the problem or the explanation and possible approaches to solutions. It requires close cooperation and complementarity, adaptation and integration of theories and methods.

The topic of this book is discussed using research gathered using a mixed-method approach. The data, both qualitative and quantitative, have been collected by interviews, a Delphi study and secondary data analysis. In the following pages, we illustrate briefly the methods used for collecting and analyzing data. The results are intertwined in the content of the different chapters.

1.2.1 Expert Interviews

As a starting point for the research, we conducted eight interviews between March and April 2018 with experts[1] from the fields of sociology, politics, anthropology, economics, futurology, consulting and human resources (HR). The experts came from the following countries: Sweden, Germany, Switzerland, Italy, France, Great Britain and the United Arab Emirates. The interviews were recorded, transcribed and evaluated using GABEK WinRelan, a PC-supported method of qualitative research and text analysis (QDA) (Zelger & Schönegger, 1994). GABEK stands for "Holistic Processing of Complexity" and is particularly suitable as an analytical method when open, unstructured data material is available. In the first step of the analysis, the data—the normal-language texts of the opinions and perceptions of the interviewees—are subdivided into coherent statements (units of meaning) and three to nine representative keywords are defined for each of these statements. The text is thus represented by a set of expressions (Buber & Kraler, 2000).

Based on keywords, the opinions and attitudes of the interviewees can be interconnected/linked with each other. Using the computer-aided software WinRelan, the data material can be visualized in network graphics or causal network graphics (Zelger, Fink, & Strickner, 2008). The systematic analysis with GABEK allows the presentation of complex phenomena and the structured analysis and presentation of data from an open, qualitative survey process (Pechlaner & Volgger, 2012).

[1] For the purpose of clarity, we will call them "interview experts" when referring to the expert interviews.

1.2.2 Delphi Study

The method is named after the ancient oracle of Delphi, which gave advice for the future. The Delphi is a structured group survey that usually consists of several rounds or can be carried out in real-time. After each round or in real-time there is an exchange of information so that the experts can correct their opinions. The procedure was founded in the 1960s at the RAND Corporation in Santa Monica, California. In a Delphi study, experts evaluate statements and future developments in their field of expertise in order to reach a consensus. The conventional Delphi is characterized by more rounds of responding; whereas in a real-time Delphi, experts can participate and interact in real-time with the other participants, comment on their answers and change them over time. The platform is activated for the participating experts in such a way that everyone can read the assessments of the other participants right from the start. It is up to the experts to decide how often they log in and review their assessments. The advantage of this form of Delphi study lies in the sovereignty of time. Delphi studies find a high acceptance in academia since they condense and objectify the opinions of many experts. Their disadvantage lies in the often-lacking conciseness, as opinions are formed that are shared by as many people as possible.

For this study, the statements for the Delphi study were defined based on the results of the interviews with the experts and the literature search. In total, the Delphi study consisted of 69 statements on 5 different topics (future of work, talents of the future, training and further education, organization of work, location factors). We opted for a Real-Time Delphi and the Calibrum software (Aengenheyster et al., 2017; Gordon & Pease, 2006). One hundred and fifteen experts from 30 countries were contacted and invited.[2] Thirty experts from 20 countries took part. They were experts from science and practice in the fields of economics, social sciences, politics, law, humanities, psychology, management and human resources. The aim was to achieve the highest possible consensus between the experts on various statements.

[2] For the purpose of clarity, we will call them "Delphi experts" when referring to the results of the Delphi survey.

1.2.3 Index

A central thread in our research was the Global Talent Competitiveness Index (GTCI) (Lanvin & Bratt, 2019; Lanvin & Evans, 2017, 2018). We used the results of the Index to identify the countries whose experts we contacted for the Delphi survey (selection of the 30 countries in the 1st percentile), for the secondary data analysis (Chap. 2) and finally for the calculation of the European Regions' Talent Competitiveness Index.

The Global Talent Competitiveness Index is an annual benchmark report that measures and ranks 119 countries and 90 cities (global cities) on their ability to attract, retain and develop talent. INSEAD the Business School for the World, the Adecco Group and TATA Communication issued its 6th report in 2019. Each year a new focus is set (e.g. Technology, entrepreneurial talents). The GTCI contains a wealth of data and indicators to help countries and decision-makers develop strategies to foster talent, bridge talent imbalances and become more competitive in the global marketplace.

In total, the GTCI contains 65 variables divided into the following 6 sections:

1. Enable (e.g. political stability, ICT infrastructure, R&D spending, labor market flexibility),
2. Attract (e.g. international students, tolerance of minorities and immigrants, brain gain, business opportunities for women),
3. Grow (e.g. tertiary enrolment, university ranking, quality of management schools, use of virtual social networks),
4. Retain (e.g. sustainability, pension system, tax system, lifestyle),
5. Vocational and technical skills (labor force with secondary education, population with secondary education, labor market productivity/workers, availability of scientists and engineers),
6. Global knowledge skills (e.g. workers with tertiary education, population with tertiary education, scientists, journal articles, innovation output).

The European Regions' Talent Competitiveness Index (Chap. 6) includes 15 indicators, subdivided into five pillars following an architecture similar to the GCTCI Model (Lanvin, Monteiro, & Bratt, 2019). The most recent data points were considered in the calculation, with 2009 as the cut-off year. Data were collected in the period between April and May 2019 from different sources where data at the regional level were available: Eurostat, the Organisation for Economic Co-operation and Development (OECD) Regional Well-Being database, publicly available rankings such as Times Higher Education World University Ranking, Numbeo and Forbes Global 2000, and national statistical bureaus.

References

Aengenheyster, S., Cuhls, K., Gerhold, L., Heiskanen-Schüttler, M., Huck, J., & Muszynska, M. (2017). Real-Time Delphi in practice – A Comparative Analysis of Existing Software-Based Tools. *Technological Forecasting and Social Change*. 118, 15–27. https://doi.org/10.1016/j.techfore.2017.01.023.

Beechler, S., & Woodward, I. C. (2009). The Global "War for Talent.". *Journal of International Management, 15*(3), 273–285. https://doi.org/10.1016/j.intman.2009.01.002.

Buber, R., & Kraler, C. (2000). How GABEK and WinRelan Support Qualitative Research. In J. Zelger & R. Buber (Eds.), *GABEK II. Zur Qualitativen Forschung. On Qualitative Research* (pp. 111–137). Innsbruck: Studien-Verlag.

Douglass, J. A., & Edelstein, R. (2009). *The Global Competition for Talent the Rapidly Changing Market for International Students and the Need for a Strategic Approach in the US* (CSHE.8.09). Berkeley. Retrieved November 10, 2019, https://cshe.berkeley.edu/publications/global-competition-talent-rapidly-changing-market-internationalstudents-and-need

Economist. (2006, October). The Battle for Brainpower. A Survey of Talent. *The Economist*. Retrieved October, 21, 2019, http://www.amrop.pl/upload/files/A_Battle_for_Brainpower._A_Survey_of_Talent.pdf

Florida, R. (2002). The Economic Geography of Talent. *Annals of the Association of American Geographers, 92*(4), 743–755. https://doi.org/10.1111/1467-8306.00314.

Gordon, T., & Pease, A. (2006). RT Delphi: An Efficient, "Round-Less" Almost Real Time Delphi Method. *Technological Forecasting and Social Change, 73*(4), 321–333. https://doi.org/10.1016/j.techfore.2005.09.005.

Lanvin, B., & Bratt, M. (2019). Growing, Attracting, and Retaining Talents at a City Level: Exploring the Local Dynamics around Entrepreneurial Talent. In

B. Lanvin & F. Monteiro (Eds.), The Global Talent Competitiveness Index 2019 (pp. 71–87). Fontainebleau: INSEAD, the Adecco Group, and Tata Communications.

Lanvin, B., & Evans, P. (2017). Country Profiles. In B. Lanvin & P. Evans (Eds.), *The Global Talent Competitiveness Index 2017: Talent and Technology* (pp. 3–34). Fontainebleau: INSEAD, the Adecco Group, and Human Capital Leadership Institute.

Lanvin, B., & Evans, P. (2018). *The Global Talent Competitiveness Index 2018: Diversity for Competitiveness*. Fontainebleau: INSEAD, the Adecco Group, and Tata Communications.

Lanvin, B., Monteiro, F., & Bratt, M. (2019). Entrepreneurial Talent for Competitiveness. In B. Lanvin & F. Monteiro (Eds.), *The Global Talent Competitiveness Index 2019* (pp. 3–37). Fontainebleau: INSEAD, the Adecco Group, and Tata Communications.

Mellander, C., & Florida, R. (2011). Creativity, Talent, and Regional Wages in Sweden. *Annals of Regional Science, 46*, 637–660. https://doi.org/10.1007/s00168-009-0354-z.

Michaels, E., Handfield-Jones, H., & Axelrod, B. (2001). *The War for Talent*. Harvard Business Review Press.

Mellander, C., & Florida, R. (2012). 'The Rise of Skills: Human Capital, the Creative Class and Regional Development The Rise of Skills: Human Capital, the Creative Class and Regional Development', CESIS Electronic Working Paper Series.

Pechlaner, H., & Volgger, M. (2012). How to Promote Cooperation in the Hospitality Industry. *International Journal of Contemporary Hospitality Management, 24*(6), 925–945. https://doi.org/10.1108/09596111211247245.

Williams, M. (2000). *The War for Talent: Getting the Best from the Best*. London: Gardners Books.

Zelger, J., Fink, S., & Strickner, J. (2008). Darstellung von Erfahrungswissen durch GABEK®. In J. Zelger, M. Raich, & P. Schober (Eds.), *GABEK III. Organisationen und ihre Wissensnetze. [Organizations and their Knowledge Nets]* (pp. 143–159). Innsbruck/Wien/München, Austria/Germany: Studien-Verlag.

Zelger, J., & Schönegger, J. (1994). *GABEK WinRelan in 12 Schritten. Ganzheitliche Bewältigung von Komplexität: Ein PC-unterstütztes Verfahren zur Wissensorganisation. [GABEK WinRelan in 12 steps. Holistic management of complexity: A PC-supported method for knowledge organization.] retrieved December 12, 2019,* http://www.iwp.jku.at/born/mpwfst/02/www.gabek.com/12steps.html.

PART I

The Future of Work: Trends

2

Global Trends Shaping the World of Work

Abstract Technology and demographic change are major trends influencing the present and future of work. Since their inception, digitization, automation and Artificial Intelligence (AI) have had an impact on work practices. While some activities and roles have been automated by machines and—increasingly—affected by algorithms, new tasks are arising and the labor market is changing. With demographic changes such as the aging and shrinking of industrialized societies and youth bulges and growing populations in emerging markets, national labor markets will be challenged. Migration, feminization and urbanization are subdevelopments affecting work. This chapter offers a macro view of current trends embracing the future of work and talents.

Keywords Global trends • Technology • Demographic change • Digitization

The future of work will be shaped by several developments. The Delphi experts have named Artificial Intelligence (AI) and digitization as central

I. Kofler et al., *The Future of High-Skilled Workers*,
https://doi.org/10.1007/978-3-030-42871-6_2

drivers affecting the labor market, along with aging society, especially for countries with a high or very high human development index (HDI). In countries with a medium or low HDI, emigration, climate change and digitization are among the main drivers. Globalization plays a role in all groups.

These trends affect the values and preferences of individuals and influence the quality and quantity of the labor force. New challenges and opportunities are coming to employers and employees. On one hand, new productive work processes can be designed and underrepresented groups such as women, migrants and older people can be supported with new possibilities and challenges. On the other hand, academic and mass literature often identifies many new risks and possible negative developments (e.g. increased unemployment).

In order to create the broadest possible picture of trends shaping the future of work while still keeping within the scope of this book, we will focus on the two major trends of digitization and demographic change. Economic, political, social and cultural aspects play decisive roles within this context and will also be included. This chapter discusses global trends at the macro level, which are then broken down to the micro level in the following chapters.

2.1 Digitization as Point of No Return

Technological innovations have always been great influence factors for work and jobs. Today we can identify four industrial transformations, which changed through the automation and digitization of labor activities and professions. The first industrial transformation introduced steam and water power for mechanical production; the second used electric power for mass production. In the third industrial revolution, technology replaced the labor force for cognitive and manual non-routine activities through the use of IT and electronics in the production process. In the fourth industrial transformation, cyber physical systems[1] should

[1] "A cyber-physical system (CPS) refers to the combination of IT, software and mechanical and electronic components that communicate via a data infrastructure such as the Internet" (Doleski & Aichele, 2014, p. 509).

independently perform tasks and make decisions. Industry 4.0 was conceived as a project of the future by various German associations, research institutions, universities and companies and is based on digitally networked processes and products, which should actively optimize production processes (Kaufmann, 2013).

The current Industry 4.0 technologies demand more workers for analytical and interactive professions. Many studies generally tend to assume that Industry 4.0 technologies further develop current roles in the working world and allow new roles to emerge (García de Soto, Agustí-Juan, Joss, & Hunhevicz, 2019). Literature debates about working conditions, educational changes, a shift in the labor markets and employment scenarios as well as the technical interface of humans and machines (Liboni, Cezarino, Jabbour, Oliveira, & Stefanelli, 2019). Scholars agree on the need for new organizational structures and business models in order to benefit from the new technologies, which require network orientation and flexibility because, according to Kaufmann, "new in Industry 4.0 is the combination of technologies to support innovative business models" (Kaufmann, 2013, p. 44; Prause & Atari, 2017).

However, Industry 4.0 is only one part of the digital transformation or digitization, which includes a broader range of changes that are often not identified in the literature. While technologies in Industry 4.0 improve and upgrade production processes, digitization plays a decisive role in differentiating corporate strategies and is decisive for value creation. In addition, digitization not only has an impact on companies, but on all disciplines, economies and industries (Szalavetz, 2019). Rather than distinguishing four industrial transformations, some scholars differentiate between the first machine age (steam power, the combustible engine, electricity etc., which mostly affected manual labor) and the second machine age (digital, robotic and computational technology, which mostly affect routine jobs) (Pouliakas, 2019).

Frey and Osborne (2013) claim that the second machine age is a critical turning point and about 47% of jobs in industrialized countries are "susceptible" to automation by new technologies. High-skilled professions are largely excluded from this. Critics complain that Frey and Osborne do not consider many factors in this study and refer only to the technical automation potential. Social, legal and ethical barriers to the implementation of new technologies are not taken into account and thus relativize the results (Bonin, Gregory, & Zierahn, 2015).

A similar study was conducted in Germany by the Leibniz Centre for European Economic Research (ZEW). Applying this Frey and Osborne' research design (2013) to Germany would indicate that 42% of workers are currently in occupations with a high probability of automation. However, the scholars who conducted this study claim that activities rather than entire occupations will be digitalized or automated. And since they don't assume that all workers in a profession are doing the same activity, while the Frey and Osborne study was used as orientation, the ZEW has chosen an alternative approach. It analyzes the probability of automation on the basis of activity structures. According to this analysis, 9% of jobs in the USA and 12% in Germany have job profiles with a high probability of automation. Here, too, the low-skilled would be particularly affected (Bonin et al., 2015).

The European Project Cedefop analyzed the impact and drivers of digital technologies on employment by surveying 49,000 EU adult workers in 28 EU Member States. Their results indicated that 43% were confronted with new technologies at work in the last four years. Such technologies include the introduction of new machines and ICT systems. One part of their study focused on the identification of determinants of "automatability risk," also using Frey and Osborne's approach (2013) as a starting point. However, with a research design adapted to European job profiles and descriptions, they concluded that about 14% of adult workers in the EU will face a very high risk of automation (Pouliakas, 2019).

These discussions about automation—also related to robotics and AI, which are considered a threat to employment with high potential for job losses—have already reached the workers, raising fears and concerns for the future of work (Lloyd & Payne, 2019). Unlike previous industrial developments, this time cognitive and non-routine jobs, which can now also be adopted by AI, are vulnerable. However, different countries are expected to be affected differently, depending on national development and industry-level institutions and structures. The experts who participated in our Delphi Study didn't find a consensus on the statement that "progressive automation and digitization in the industrialized countries results in a massive increase in unemployment, especially among the low-skilled" but agreed that "AI may be thought of as a radically different mechanism for wealth creation" (72.93% consensus).

Transformative and destructive digitalization may affect jobs and occupations in various ways. A highly present scenario in recent studies in economic and sociology fields predicts that technologies associated with robotics and AI will replace many jobs with only a few new roles created. The McKinsey Global Institute speaks of 50% of jobs in the USA and UK that will be automated in the near future (Bughin, Manyika, & Woetzel, 2017). A study from Frey and Osborne (2017) focused mainly on destructive effects and revealed that in the USA, jobs face either a very high or very low risk of destructive digitalization, with very few at mid-level risk.

The project from Fossen and Sorgner (2019) focuses especially on the difference between transformative and destructive effects on occupation. They categorized four major groups, based on the extent to which transformative and destructive digitalization have an effect. The first group is "human terrain" occupations, upon which both destructive and transformative digitalization have a low impact. Jobs such as customer service representatives, janitors and cleaners, teaching assistants, funeral attendants, graders and sorters (agriculture) belong to this group. Approximately 12% of workers can be considered "human terrain" and they remain largely unaffected by digitization. The second group is called "collapsing occupations," upon which the destructive effects of digitalization have a high impact and transformative effects have a low impact. These include occupations such as cashiers, retail salespeople, office clerks, servers, secretaries, bookkeepers, accounting assistants, security guards, models, telemarketers and so forth. About 37–38% are employed in this category. They require no or very low levels of creativity and social intelligence, which makes it quite easy to digitalize them. Low effects of destructive digitalization but high levels of transformative digitalization face the third group, called "rising stars." In contrast to the second group, creativity and social intelligence are in demand in these professions and are thus very hard to replace by machines. Jobs like nurses, general and operational managers, elementary school teachers, maintenance and repair workers, physicists, surgeons, pilots, dentists and so forth belong to this group (37–38%). The last group "machine terrain" is characterized by high levels of transformative and destructive digitalization effects. These jobs require relatively high levels of manual skills, but AI puts these jobs at risk of being replaced in the long run. Eleven percent of workers are employed in this group, which includes accountants, auditors, executive secretaries, executive administration assistants, heavy truck drivers and so forth (Fossen & Sorgner, 2019).

In general, techno-optimists and -pessimists discuss the implications of a jobless future rather than go a step back to verify such scenarios. In addition, politicians seem to spread the fear of robots and digitalization taking human jobs over and making human work superfluous in a fast-approaching future.

However, this discussion is anything but new. As far back as the 1930s, John Maynard Keynes wrote that machines will abolish human labor within two generations (Maynard Keynes, 1930). Indeed, history has shown that every major change or industrial revolution has fundamentally changed the labor market, but not in a mostly destructive way. In fact, many new jobs and activities have emerged that one simply could not imagine before (Fleming, 2019; Zürcher, 2017). People have never become superfluous; they have adapted to the new conditions and have created new jobs and new opportunities in the labor market. For instance, some researchers argue that AI and robots will coexist for some time with conventional structures and then new roles will emerge on different levels and the job variability will become higher (García de Soto et al., 2019).

This assumption has been confirmed by our Delphi experts. We found 72.12% consensus on the statement that "digitization tends to create more new jobs than replace existing ones." Additionally, the experts didn't find a consensus on the statement that "with the progressive improvement of artificial intelligence (and the increasing autonomy of machines) it is to be expected that demanding mental work will also be taken over by the computers."

2.2 Demographic Change: The Elephant in the Room

As mentioned previously, in addition to technological innovations, demographic change in its various forms also plays a central role as a driver for the labor market and especially for talent management.

On one hand, in industrialized economies people are becoming older (the Organisation for Economic Co-operation and Development [OECD] average life expectancy is 80 years; in 1960 it was ten years less) and show low fertility rates, which leads to populations shrinking with a subsequent decrease in the working population. This will be a headwind to national and global growth. Many countries implemented policy movements that increase the retirement age as life expectancy has risen rapidly over the last decades in Western countries.

On the other hand, developing countries show a high population growth, averagely young people and high fertility rates. Experts from our Delphi Study showed a high consensus (77.3%) that the high-population, high-growth, emerging markets such as China and India have a great influence on the European labor market.

These contradictory developments also influence the labor market for the highly qualified. Research in Global Talent Management (GTM) and International Human Resource Management (IHRM) examined the challenge of current demographic trends with regard to the changing workforce demographics. Scholars examined how organizations attract, select and retain different generations of talents: older or mature workers and younger workers (Tarique & Schuler, 2010).

However, at the moment, the focus on organization by many GTM studies is limiting their scope, because the macro view is fundamental to global talent management. For example, "as a result of demographic change, the number of Americans and Europeans in the world population is shrinking. The majority of highly skilled people will not come from the highly industrialized countries of the West in the future." This statement has been agreed on by a consensus of 75% in our Delphi study. Therefore, talent flows related to migration across countries, different population structures and dynamics are influence factors that should be considered (Khilji, Tarique, & Schuler, 2015). In fact, as mentioned above, developing and emerging economies are experiencing the greatest growth globally. Within the next few decades, more than 50% of the global population growth will be concentrated in nine countries, of whom eight are developing states (India, Nigeria, Pakistan, The Democratic Republic of the Congo, Ethiopia, the United Republic of Tanzania, Indonesia, Egypt and the USA) (DESA, UN, 2019).

We identified three sub-areas of demographic development that influence the labor market in general and talent management in particular: feminization, urbanization and migration.

2.2.1 Women in Pole Position?

Women could take a key role in the design of demographic change, because they represent an important part of labor market participation and thus influence production and the economic performance of a country. In particular, countries that attract talent have the potential to intervene more and support women in education as well as career opportunities, thereby compensating for problems caused by demographic change.

The Delphi experts tend to agree that the world of work is being feminized, which has a noticeable influence on the labor market and/or work processes (72.48% consensus). In general, it is noted that due to social, legal and cultural norms and trends, which determine whether women's activities are regarded as economic or not, the estimated value of the female labor force has generally been lower than that of the male. The generally lower participation of women in the labor market is also connected to the fact that they have long assumed the traditional role of homemakers and mothers. Thus, they are more often involved in work without pay in family enterprises, work on farms or other work in or near their homes, especially in low-income countries (Addabbo, Rodríguez-Modroño, & Muñoz, 2015; Lundberg, 1985; Tano, 1993). Recently, the International Labour Organization (ILO) noted that the worldwide female labor force participation rate has decreased on a global level, from 51.9% in 1990 to 47.7% in 2015 (The World Bank, 2019).

However, in high-income countries, although women are increasingly acquiring higher education, inequalities in accessing well-paying occupations are still found in many jobs and countries around the world, especially in higher positions. Actually, female labor participation presents an opportunity for companies to attract and retain talented women to help fill talent gaps. Furthermore, even though scholars show that companies with a higher representation of women in executive positions perform sustainably better than companies with proportionally fewer women at the top, little has changed in the number of executive women in companies in recent years. In fact, especially in technology, research and development occupations, the gender gap is still high. The proportion of women in management positions at large international companies underlines this gap. Women account for 25% of executive staff at Microsoft, 26% at Google, 27% at Amazon, 29% at Apple and 33% at Facebook (Richter, 2020).

This apparent gap suggests that women still do not represent a decisive percentage of the highly skilled at a global level. One part of the secondary data analysis regarding the Global Talent Competitive Index (GTCI) (see introduction) suggests no positive correlation with the actual participation of women in the labor market. In other words, a high participation of women in the labor market of a country does not imply a higher GTCI.

Secondary Data Analysis: Correlations GTCI and Demographic Variables

In order to shed light on the demographic aspect of talent management and to show how important demographic policies are for talent management at national and regional level, various correlations were calculated on the basis of the GTCI.

The demographic data were collected from official sources UN/DESA, ILO and World Development Indicators for the year 2015 of the 118 countries included in the GTCI.

In the GTCI, the rankings of the overall and individual dimensions as well as the percentages were included in the calculations. Since the GTCI Report of 2017 concentrates largely on data from 2015, this report is used as a reference.

Using the software SPSS, the Shapiro-Wilk test identified the Kendall-Tau-b and Spearman as correlation analyses. The Kruskal-Wallis test additionally checked the correlations.

2.2.2 The Clustering of Talent in Global Cities

The second aspect at the macro level that is relevant for the labor market of highly qualified people is urbanization. For the first time, since 2008 more people live in urban areas than in rural areas. Moreover, talents are found more often in cities and urban areas than in rural areas.

Cities in all parts of the world adopted proactive strategies to attract the highly skilled or talents. Global mega events such as the Olympic Games, World Expos and World Championships are strong branding strategies which also promote living in cities (Lanvin & Evans, 2017). Cities are more manageable, agile and thus able to produce innovation much faster than rural areas or national entities. Tightly connected ecosystems, as can typically be found in cities or small countries where the government, business and education collaborate closely because they are geographically close, are able to identify and deliver solutions rapidly (Lanvin & Evans, 2017). Furthermore, according to their GTCI Report in 2017, "Cities and regions are often better positioned than countries to develop and brand features such as quality of life and educational opportunities that are attractive to both domestic and international talent" (p. 101).

The concentration of talents can lead to innovation and economic growth. For example, there are particular cities where certain industries are concentrated: the film industry in Hollywood; new technology, robotics and AI in Silicon Valley; the former automobile industry in Detroit and so forth. According to Florida (2003) "the ability to rapidly mobilize talent from such a concentration of people is a tremendous source of competitive advantage for companies in our time-driven economy of the creative age" (p. 5). The positive correlation between a high degree of urbanization and a high GTCI emphasizes this statement. Chapter 5 discusses further urbanization in relation to location factors in detail.

2.2.3 Migration in Aging and Shrinking Societies

Migration also needs to be discussed in relation to demographic changes, labor and, especially, talents. In OECD countries it is noticeable that the level of education of migrants continuously increased in the past decades. Between 2000/2001 and 2015/2016, high-skilled migrants born outside of an OECD country and residing in the OECD rose from 27% to 35%. Meanwhile, the proportion of poorly educated migrants not born in an OECD country but residing in an OECD countries decreased from 38% to less than 30% (OECD, 2019). It is no big surprise that small developing countries are mostly affected by high-skilled emigration or a brain drain (OECD, 2019). In fact, a large number of high-skilled migrants to the OECD come from Asian countries such as India, China and the Philippines (Bailey & Mulder, 2017).

As we've seen above, demographic change is a challenge for the economic performance of many industrialized countries particularly due to a shortage of workers. Immigration is now seen by many countries as an important opportunity to address this shortage and to sustain economic growth. Experts from our Delphi study also confirmed these perspectives, with a 74.58% consensus on the statement that "the highly industrialized countries of the West will be characterized by a shrinking population and ageing and smaller labor markets where, without external immigration, there will be an acute shortage of highly skilled workers and high unemployment among the low-skilled." Several researchers also noticed and documented the importance of expected income differentials for motivating international migration (Borjas, 1990; Harris & Todaro, 1970; Hatton & Williamson, 2002; Mayda, 2010). According to Westmore (2014), the skill-specific wage differential of destination countries and origin countries is crucial for the migration decision.

Worldwide education has improved dramatically in the last decades and the pool of tertiary-educated and highly qualified people is getting bigger and bigger. Policies differentiate between high-skilled migration and low-skilled migration. Low-skilled migration is often seen as a problem for societies, while high-skilled migration needs to be promoted. Industrialized countries are implementing policies to attract people from third world countries and also from the Global South, and developing and emerging economies have started to formulate policies to retain and attract native high-skilled workers (Czaika, 2018). National strategies and policies targeting highly skilled migrants led to a global competition for talents and the highly skilled (Boeri, Brücker, Docquier, & Rapoport, 2012; Czaika, 2018). In fact, countries with a high GTCI show a high percentage of migration stock and thus display a positive correlation.

Migration is a fundamental issue in the future of global talents and will be discussed again in Chap. 5.

The European Union, for instance, regards immigration as a compensation for the declining workforce and overburdening of social security systems in most EU member states. Therefore, as early as 2007 it became a priority for the European Commission to develop a new policy on legal migration. While for citizens of EU countries there are no restrictions within the EU, many migration programs focus on so-called third country nationals (TCNs) (Bailey & Mulder, 2017).These aim to "keep Europe an attractive destination for migrants in a time of demographic decline, through actions such as reviewing the Blue Card scheme, re-prioritizing integration policies, and making migration policy work better for countries of origin, for example by easing remittances" (Marinescu, 2017, p. 7).

Long before the EU began to address this issue, countries such as the USA, Canada, Australia and the UK had already introduced such programs to attract and retain talent. Highly skilled migrants in particular are attractive for nations, which can lead to a mobility gap (see Chap. 5) (Bailey & Mulder, 2017; Czaika, 2018). In general, recent studies indicate that research often considers only the human capital perspective. Bailey and Mulder (2017) refer to three aspects of this issue that have been neglected but need more attention. First, talents are not only human capital or economic agents, but are social, cultural and political actors with different backgrounds. Second, life-course choices of highly skilled migrants shape their future and their lives are linked to their significant others. Third, studies mostly ignored the institutional and employer focus and aspect.

In fact, one issue that can be identified by studying migration policies to attract the highly skilled is that their dominant image and policy focus are men, while women are seen as co-movers (Bailey & Mulder, 2017; Czaika, 2018). As we saw above, social and cultural aspects are often ignored in relation to this issue, in the policy discourse as well as in academic literature. This imbalance should be considered in future studies because, as mentioned previously, the female labor force is essential for economic performance and thus must be included in the discussion regarding the highly skilled.

2.3 Conclusion

In sum, we introduced two global trends, with their various subsections, which are crucial for the future of work and the high-skilled. Even though technological progress and digitization is often regarded as a panopticon gaze that silently oversees societies, it might not have as much impact as feared on unemployment rates in the future. In other words, labor will probably not become extinct in the next few decades, but technological innovations will influence current job profiles and activities and create new ones. The next chapter discusses, among other things, what skills are needed in the future to adapt best to new technologies and the implications of a skills mismatch.

The second trend, demographic change, includes several interconnected subtrends. The aging and in some cases shrinking population of the industrialized economies and the young and expanding populations of developing and emerging countries lead to different migration flows. The highly skilled in particular have greater opportunities to migrate, while low-skilled workers are often seen as a burden for social systems. Furthermore, people have a higher tendency to move and live in cities, globally speaking. This is another mobility form. Issues such as female labor, female labor migration, the social and cultural backgrounds of labor migrants, the institutional focus and so forth are rarely discussed in the literature and require more research.

Although technology and digitization can be considered separate from migration, they also influence each other and are interconnected, particularly regarding work. For example, activities are often digitized where no or not enough human workers are found or where human capital is too expensive. On the other hand, expensive workers are often replaced by cheaper immigrant workers. In this case, jobs and activities are not digitized, because immigrants are more convenient for the companies. For instance, while in Japan, the country with one of the oldest populations in the world, care robots are already being implemented to combat labor shortages in care professions, in many European countries there is a similar shortage, but it is cheaper to solve the problem through immigration. This example shows a fundamental link that science and practice should take into account, although there are, of course, more factors involved.

References

Addabbo, T., Rodríguez-Modroño, P., & Muñoz, L. G. (2015). Gender Differences in Labor Force Participation Rates in Spain and Italy Under the Great Recession. *Revista de Economia Mundial*, 41: 21–42.

Bailey, A., & Mulder, C. H. (2017). Highly Skilled Migration Between the Global North and South: Gender, Life Courses and Institutions. *Journal of Ethnic and Migration Studies, 43*(16), 2689–2703. https://doi.org/10.1080/1369183X.2017.1314594.

Boeri, T., Brücker, H., Docquier, F., & Rapoport, H. (2012). Brain Drain and Brain Gain: The Global Competition to Attract High-Skilled Migrants. Oxford: Oxford University Press. https://doi.org/10.1093/acprof:oso/9780199654826.001.0001.

Bonin, H., Gregory, T., & Zierahn, U. (2015). *Übertragung der Studie von Frey/Osborne (2013) auf Deutschland* [Transfer of the study from Frey/Osborne (2013) to Germany]. Mannheim: ZEW.

Borjas, G. J. (1990). *Friends or Strangers: The Impact of Immigrants on the US Economy*. New York: Basic Books.

Bughin, J., Manyika, J., & Woetzel, J. (2017). *Jobs Lost, Jobs Gained: Workforce Transitions in a Time of Automation*. McKinsey Global Institute, 150. https://doi.org/10.1002/lary.20616.

Czaika, M. (2018). *High-Skilled Migration: Drivers and Policies*. Oxford: Oxford University Press. https://doi.org/10.1093/oso/9780198815273.001.0001.

DESA, U.N. (2019). *World Population Prospects 2019: Highlights*. New York: United Nations Department for Economic and Social Affairs.

Doleski, O. D., & Aichele, C. (2014). Idee des intelligenten Energiemarktkonzepts [Idea of the intelligent energy market concept]. In C. Aichele & O. D. Doleski (Eds.), *Smart Market. Vom Smart Grid zum intelligenten Energiemarkt*, (pp. 3–51). Wiesbaden: Springer Vieweg. https://doi.org/10.1007/978-3-658-02778-0_1.

Fleming, P. (2019). Robots and Organization Studies: Why Robots Might Not Want to Steal Your Job. *Organization Studies*, 40(1), 23-38. https://doi.org/10.1177/0170840618765568.

Florida, R. (2003). *The Rise of the Creative Class: And How It's Transforming Work, Leisure, Community, and Everyday Life*. New York: Basic Books.

Fossen, F., & Sorgner, A. (2019). Mapping the Future of Occupations: Transformative and Destructive Effects of New Digital Technologies on Jobs.

Foresight and STI Governance, 13(2), 10–18. https://doi.org/10.17323/25002597.2019.2.10.18.
Frey, C. B., & Osborne, M. (2013). The Future of Employment. *Oxford Martin Programme on Technology and Employment*. Retrieved November 11, 2019, from http://sep4u.gr/wp-content/uploads/The_Future_of_Employment_ox_2013.pdf
Frey, C. B., & Osborne, M. A. (2017). The Future of Employment: How Susceptible Are Jobs to Computerisation? *Technological Forecasting and Social Change, 114*, 254–280. https://doi.org/10.1016/j.techfore.2016.08.019.
García de Soto, B., Agustí-Juan, I., Joss, S., & Hunhevicz, J. (2019). Implications of Construction 4.0 to the Workforce and Organizational Structures. *International Journal of Construction Management*, 1–13. https://doi.org/10.1080/15623599.2019.1616414.
Harris, J. R., & Todaro, M. P. (1970). Migration, Unemployment and Development: A Two-Sector Analysis. *The American Economic Review, 60*(1), 126–142.
Hatton, T. J., & Williamson, J. G. (2002). *What Fundamentals Drive World Migration?* In National Bureau of Economic Research (Cambridge, MA), Working Paper 9159.
Kaufmann, T. (2013). *Geschäftsmodelle in Industrie 4.0 und dem Internet der Dinge: der Weg vom Anspruch in die Wirklichkeit* [Business models in Industry 4.0 and the Internet of Things: the path from claim to reality]. Wiesbaden: Springer-Verlag.
Khilji, S. E., Tarique, I., & Schuler, R. S. (2015). Incorporating the Macro View in Global Talent Management. *Human Resource Management Review, 25*(3), 236–248. https://doi.org/10.1016/j.hrmr.2015.04.001.
Lanvin, B., & Evans, P. (2017). *The Global Talent Competitiveness Index 2017: Talent and Technology* (B. Lanvin & P. Evans, Eds.). Fontainebleau.
Liboni, L. B., Cezarino, L. O., Jabbour, C. J. C., Oliveira, B. G., & Stefanelli, N. O. (2019). Smart Industry and the Pathways to HRM 4.0: Implications for SCM. *Supply Chain Management: An International Journal, 24*(1), 124–146. https://doi.org/10.1108/SCM-03-2018-0150.
Lloyd, C., & Payne, J. (2019). Rethinking Country Effects: Robotics, AI and Work Futures in Norway and the UK. *New Technology, Work and Employment, 34*(3), 208–225. https://doi.org/10.1111/ntwe.12149.
Lundberg, S. (1985). The Added Worker Effect. *Journal of Labour Economics, 3*(1), 11–37.
Marinescu, N. (Ed.). (2017). *East-West Migration in the European Union*. Newcastle: Cambridge Scholars Publishing.

Mayda, A. M. (2010). International migration: A panel data analysis of the determinants of bilateral flows. *Journal of Population Economics*, 23(4), 1249–1274.

Maynard Keynes, J. (1930). Economic Possibilities for our Grandchildren. *Essays in Persuasion*. New York: Harcourt Brace (1932), (pp. 358–373).

OECD. (2019). The New Immigrants Global Trends in Migration Towards OECD Countries Between 2000/01 and 2015/16. Retrieved November 25, 2019, from Migration Data Brief N°4 June website: https://www.oecd.org/migration/mig/Migration-data-brief-4-EN.pdf

Pouliakas, K. (2019). *Automation Risk in the EU Labour Market. A Skill-Needs Approach* (No. 11829). IZA discussion papers. Retrieved January 24, 2020 from IZA website: https://www.iza.org/publications/dp/11829/determinants-of-automation-risk-in-the-eu-labour-market-a-skills-needs-approach.

Prause, G., & Atari, S. (2017). On Sustainable Production Networks for Industry 4.0. *Entrepreneurship and Sustainability Issues, 4*(4), 421–431. https://doi.org/10.9770/jesi.2017.4.4(2).

Richter, F. (2020). GAFAM: Women Still Underrepresented in Tech. Retrieved May 11, 2020, from statista website: https://www.statista.com/chart/4467/female-employees-at-tech-companies/.

Szalavetz, A. (2019). Digitalisation, Automation and Upgrading in Global Value Chains – Factory Economy Actors Versus Lead Companies. *Post-Communist Economies*, 31(5), 646–670. https://doi.org/10.1080/14631377.2019.1578584.

Tano, D. K. (1993). The Added Worker Effect: A Causality Test. *Economic Letters, 43*(1), 111–117.

Tarique, I., & Schuler, R. S. (2010). Global Talent Management: Literature Review, Integrative Framework, and Suggestions for Further Research. *Journal of World Business, 45*, 122–133. https://doi.org/10.1016/j.jwb.2009.09.019.

The World Bank. (2019). Labor Force Participation Rate, Female (% of Female Population Ages 15+) (Modeled ILO Estimate). Retrieved November 18, 2019, from worldbank website https://data.worldbank.org/indicator/sl.tlf.cact.fe.zs?end=2019&start=1990

Westmore, B. (2014). *International Migration: The Relationship with Economic and Policy Factors in the Home and Destination Country* (No. 1140). https://doi.org/10.1787/5jz123h8nd7l-en.

Zürcher, B. (2017). The End of Work. In B. S. Frey & D. Iselin (Eds.), *Economic Ideas You Should Forget*, (pp. 163–164). https://doi.org/10.1007/978-3-319-47458-8_71.

3

The Jungle of Skills Mismatch

Abstract In the knowledge economy there is an increased focus on skills. Moreover, rapidly changing developments and growing skills shortages are generating considerable political and socio-economic tensions. The workers with the greatest potential value on the labor market seem to be the high-skilled workers, with strong digital and technological skills and complex thinking. This may have an important economic impact, but research shows that a skills shortage is not the only problem—there is also a problem of a skills mismatch with implications at different levels. These developments also have an impact on future generations—on the skills that are important for the talents of tomorrow and what that means for the education system.

Keywords Skills mismatch • Talents • Future developments

The rapid technological advances and societal changes described in Chap. 2 are affecting not only the organization and institutions of work but also workers at the individual level, influencing the skills and competencies

I. Kofler et al., *The Future of High-Skilled Workers*,
https://doi.org/10.1007/978-3-030-42871-6_3

needed and demanded on the labor market. The so-called skills revolution (Mellander & Florida, 2012) implies that since 1990s there has been an increased focus on skills because of the transition from an industrial economy to an economy based on knowledge, innovation and skills, known as the knowledge economy.

While the face of work is changing, the skills and competencies demanded of the workforce are changing too (Burke & Ng, 2006; OECD, 2017; WEF, 2018). These are not limited to specific working skills: innovative and changing organizational strategies also have expectations of engaged and involved workers, demanding more flexibility, performance and productivity. On the one hand, this means that the entire education and training system is under pressure to adapt to these requirements. On the other hand, in addition to the apparent shortage of skilled and highly skilled workers, many European countries complain of a growing polarization between the supply and demand sides of the required skills. This gap between the skills required and skills offered in the labor market is referred to as the skills mismatch. Hence, the discussion about skills and competencies is both a subjective and a societal phenomenon concerning political, economic and educational institutions.

In general, high-skilled workers are associated with a growing and prospering economy (Bertoli, Brücker, Facchini, Mayda, & Peri, 2009; Mellander & Florida, 2012; Rathelot & Van Rens, 2017). Hence, a capitalistic Western system will always have a high demand for talents because such a system has a primary intention of economic growth. Additionally, the current structural transformation that society is undergoing—through globalization, demographic change, digitization and automation—is considerably changing the labor market institutions. Businesses are increasingly complaining of a shortage of skilled workers, while certain countries and professions are affected differently.

In Europe, data show a growing skills shortage and mismatch (Brunello & Wruuck, 2019) followed by several political measures in order to overcome the problem. In relation to politics and economy, a skills shortage—particularly a shortage of highly skilled workers—may negatively affect the entire economic system, because it can hinder labor productivity and innovation. In the USA, Beaudry (2016) shows that after 2000 there was a weakening of the demand for cognitive skills and a simultaneous growth in the supply of highly educated people, with the consequence of overeducation in many jobs.

On an individual level, this means that workers either do not meet the right requirements or are under- or over-qualified for their job, with consequences on their wages and on their subjective and psychological situation. A skills mismatch or gap can therefore have considerable economic and social costs for society as a whole. This chapter will give an overview of the literature on both the structural and individual levels of the skills mismatch. Finally, there will be an assessment of future requirements and what this means for future generations.

3.1 Skills Shortage, Skills Mismatch, Skills Gap: A General Confusion of Concepts

It is not a new phenomenon, especially for firms, that workers do not have the requested skills and education for the demands of jobs (Handel, 2003). The scale has changed over time, but the arguments remain the same: from overeducation to a mismatch between low- and high-skilled workers to a decline of high school and tertiary educated people. Technological change, such as the structural changes of the information economy and the wide spread of the internet, has been an important contributor to the discussion. There is a substantial change in the way professional profiles are conceived, no longer characterized only by a strong technical specialization but oriented more through hybrid forms, in which the technical component is integrated with the relational and business components. The demand for skills is therefore moving toward a model that combines technical-specialist skills with relational skills such as problem-solving, the flexibility to interface with multiple disciplines and the ability to adapt to changing organizational contexts.

It is difficult both to frame the problem and to find an unambiguous definition of skills mismatch. It is difficult both to frame the problem and to find an unambiguous definition of skills mismatch. Considering all the developments and profound changes, there are different forms of skills mismatch referring to many types of discrepancies between the skills offered and needed on the labor market. In a broad sense, the skills mismatch is defined as the gap between individual skills and the skills needed in or for the labor market. However, scholars and also the OECD define different concepts of a skills mismatch, because there are different manifestations, measures, determinants and consequences of a mismatch that can be experienced either by employees, employers or at firm level. They identified six different concepts:

- skills shortage (the demand exceeds the supply of a specific skill);
- skills gap (skills are different from those required for a specific job);
- vertical mismatch (level of education is less or more than required for a specific job);
- horizontal mismatch (type of education is inappropriate); over- or undereducation (more or less education than required);
- over- or underqualification (higher or lower qualification than required for a specific job);
- skills obsolescence (previous skills no longer required)

In policy debates the concept is used in a very broad sense and incorporates a variety of phenomena, even if their manifestations and consequences are very different. For employers, the skills gap has different definition to that of economic scientists or politicians. Regarding reports from the chamber of commerce or trade associations, for example (Unioncamere, 2019), employers list different tasks and skills they "need" in order to improve performance, while economists refer to the costs and benefits of specific skills. Firms are only willing to pay for the skills that they need. If employers cannot find workers with the desired skills who are willing to work for the wage they are offering, then they consider that a skills gap (Mehta, 2016). Therefore, an economic approach to overcoming the skills gap would be to identify the benefits and costs of a specific skills supply, and the definition of a skills gap would be that the cost of investment in skills exceeds the overall benefits/returns.

Effectively, one of the main issues highlighted in the literature is that skills and competencies are difficult to measure. The most common skill proxies to measure mismatch or shortage are qualification, years of education and the type of occupation. The different concepts above show that there aren't statistically adequate measures that can provide an objective overview of the situation, that is, when education is used as a measure to identify under- and overqualification, this does not consider other skills necessary for a specific job.

As we demonstrated that there is a misleading misunderstanding of the definition and measurement of skills mismatch, the question arises—where is the real problem of skills mismatch? There are different positions among scholars and policy makers. A large body of research shows the costs of overeducation and human capital, but policies continue to focus on skills shortages and gaps even though the evidence shows the contrary (Cedefop, 2018; Handel, 2003; McGuinness, Pouliakas, & Redmond, 2018; Mehta, 2016; Rathelot & Van Rens, 2017; Seils, 2018; Sutherland, 2012; Voth, 2017). Voth (2017) summarizes it as "There is no such thing as a skill shortage. Forget about that. It's about wages that are too low" (p. 157). Wages are not rising in order to balance supply and demand, while high-skilled people are underpaid in some jobs or are leaving their country. So, the problem of the brain drain comes with considerable costs. In Italy, for example, it is calculated at 14 billion euro: in 2017 more than half of the 115,000 Italians who emigrated had a medium to high qualification (Tortuga, 2019).

While the majority of research focuses on overeducation and overskilling (Brunello & Wruuck, 2019; McGuinness et al., 2018; Seils, 2018; Unioncamere, 2019), the European skills and jobs (ESJ) survey, a survey on skills mismatch in all European Member States carried out by The European Centre for the Development of Vocational Training (Cedefop), is considered an exception, because it includes a variety of measures captured in different times (Cedefop, 2016, 2018). The survey shows that about 30% of European employees do not have qualifications that match their positions and 45% of the workers are not satisfied with the utilization of their skills at work. One of the main results of the survey is that there is an existing skills mismatch in Europe, foremost in terms of overqualification that suggests that underutilization of human capital or wage issues is more of a problem than human capital deficit (McGuinness et al., 2018; Sutherland, 2012; Voth, 2017).

Consequently, policy makers should pay more attention to the real problem and develop their policies based on evidence on the supply and demand side and the surplus of (underutilized) human capital rather than focusing on shortages. McGuinness et al. (2018) also analyzed several policy documents and discovered that there is a broad definition of skills mismatch and policy recommendations focus primarily on skill shortages. There is, as seen before, a substantial difference between the two, and it is problematic for the measurement and the interpretation of skills shortages statistics if they are only based on employer surveys. Politics and policies are needed to match jobs with the requested skills more effectively based on evidence-based data of the actual situation in order to find a greater balance and eliminate gaps in human productivity.

The current situation is not only indicative of a divergence between evidence and policies, but also leads to other related issues. One is migration, high-skilled migration in particular. Today we observe that migrants in general are younger and often more educated than locals. In general, there is a rise in secondary- and tertiary-educated people and the increase in supply of the high-skilled is partly also driven by rising educational aspirations. Moreover, educated people have a higher propensity to migrate than the less educated (Mathias Czaika, 2017). At the same time, there is a growth in policies addressing high-skilled migration in order to overcome the skills shortage. This shows that politics has an interest in responding to the skills shortage with a selected skill migration policy, guided by the idea mentioned previously that skilled workers can bring positive externalities and effects on the economy.

Other phenomena affecting the labor market are job polarization—a general growth in the share of the highest and lowest paid jobs at the expense of middle-wage jobs (Salvatori, 2018) and, closely linked, job segregation by skill, dividing regions into low-skills or knowledge-intensive industries. High-skilled migrants tend to move toward urban environments or to global cities (Sassen, 2005), with a higher cultural diversity leading to an unequal distribution between urban and rural areas of skills distribution. Another aggregate level is that the immigration of high-skilled workers (if they cost less than the native workers) tends to lower the wages of high-skilled locals because for firms it is easier to hire a cheaper high-skilled migrant than to adjust wages (Voth, 2017).

In general, it is difficult to come to fixed conclusions about the phenomenon of skills mismatch because of the problems of measurement, the different positions within research and politics, and the implications and consequences of a skills mismatch on job polarization, segregation and migration. What is certain is that ongoing megatrends will put pressure on the important European Union economies of the future. Increasing technological development together with population aging will result in a greater importance of technological skills.

Important factors that must also be considered are the changing value systems of future generations and increasing insecurity in future developments in general. The following section will address the individual level, looking at who the talents of tomorrow are and what skills will be expected from them.

3.2 The Talents of Tomorrow and Their Skills

In the "Skills Strategy 2019," the OECD (2019b) argues, that the "skills-issue" will become increasingly important for economic growth because of megatrends that will bring considerable changes—demography, globalization, technology and migration. The highly interconnected and rapidly changing world will demand that workers be highly flexible, developing new skills throughout their working life. For this reason, policies supporting the development of the "right" skills can help to overcome challenges in the labor market.

The Program for the International Assessment of Adult Competencies (PIAAC) data show that there is a high and positive correlation between skills and labor market outcome: the higher the skills, the higher the chance of getting a job and getting higher wages (OECD, 2019b). Moreover, this research also shows that people with higher skills are also more likely to participate in democratic processes and community life, and to have better health. Countries where people educate themselves throughout their lives and use their skills effectively at work and in society are more productive, more innovative and offer a higher quality of life.

Technological developments are one of the main drivers of rapid change. Technology, digitization, automation and artificial intelligence can deeply change professions and, consequently, the skills required. They can both replace jobs and create new jobs: over the last 15 years, automation has created about four times as many jobs as it has replaced (UK) (Insall & Borthakur, 2015). The main changes in jobs are related to how routine the tasks are and the skills required. High knowledge-based professions are also starting to change, for example medical jobs, where artificial intelligence is expected to have a relevant role in the future.

In more developed countries, we are currently observing a growth in both the highest and lowest paid jobs at the expense of middle-wage jobs, which are declining in all OECD countries (OECD, 2019a). However, although middle-skilled jobs are declining and high-skilled jobs growing, the share of middle-wage jobs has increased and the share of high-wage jobs has not grown in proportion to high-skilled occupations, and workers with less than tertiary education are shifting toward low-skilled occupations (OECD, 2019a).

Another phenomenon linked to qualification-related structural change that has not received much attention up to now is workplace segregation by skill: labor demand is increasingly divided into firms (and regions) hiring predominantly low-skilled workers, or knowledge-intensive industries and services recruiting the highly skilled. This will produce inequalities between urban and rural realities, because most technological and computer-related jobs appear mainly in urban areas, where most of the highly skilled are living (OECD, 2017). High-skilled talents contribute to the ability of a city, a country or a region to be innovative and adopt new technologies in order to be more productive and grow. The challenge for policies and countries that are less innovative is to attract and retain talents to boost their economy and innovation activity and to update the skills of existing talents.

Many studies underline the impact that technology, automation and digitalization will have on the labor market. Jobs in the IT sector will be the most requested with education following. Demographic change also has an impact: in industrialized countries there will be big growth in all jobs around the care sector as the population gets older. In our Delphi study, the experts identified the following skills as being the most important in the future (ranking from the most important to the least):

- Specific job-related expertise and skills
- Innovation and creativity
- Effective communication skills
- Commitment to deliver
- Positive energy/attitude
- Decision-making skills
- Capacity for teamwork
- Potential for growth and development
- An entrepreneurial spirit

One section in our Delphi study was titled "Talents of tomorrow" (see Table 3.1). We wanted to know who those talents are and what kind of skills they must learn. One key statement, which reached a consensus of 85.63%, was: "The activities of certain professions will change considerably as a result of digitization and automation, making job profiles appear completely different and creating new job profiles." Several also predicted

Table 3.1 Main results from the Delphi study: section "Talents of tomorrow" (own elaboration)

	Agreement
The activities of certain professions will change considerably as a result of digitization and automation, making job profiles appear completely different and creating new job profiles.	85.63%
New professions will emerge that require far more creativity and flexibility than many of today's professions.	82.27%
Social skills, such as teamwork and communication skills, are becoming increasingly important.	82.05%
Due to the increasing flexibility of work organization, entrepreneurial skills and project management skills will gain in importance.	76.37%
IT activities and skills, both at a professional level and in day-to-day use, will be required by more than 80% of the workforce.	76.13%
	Disagreement
The professional position is losing its importance in terms of social status.	60.15%
Tomorrow's highly skilled and creative workers will not differ significantly from those of today.	54.96%

that the kind of jobs that we know today wouldn't exist in 30 years. One important impact, as seen above, is that many activities will be replaced by true automation technologies. These wouldn't change the profession as such, but the job structure will need to be adapted and adjusted and humans will increasingly perform jobs and activities that are difficult to automate, while machines will take over activities that are easy to automate. Also, communication technologies will have an impact on decentralizing, outsourcing and offshoring, shifting jobs to others or to the consumers.

Technological development and progress will reshape most occupations, but moreover, job tasks will be altered. As high-skilled jobs are increasing, but not high-paid jobs, it is probably because all those structural changes are demanding high-level cognitive and complex skills (such as written and oral expression, reasoning and complex problem-solving), social interactions and adaptations skills. Foremost, as the experts agree, "social skills, such as teamwork and communication skills, are becoming increasingly important." Even if the jobs, tasks and skills of tomorrow will change, some skills, for example soft skills, are important both now and in the future. The education system will be asked to focus on those transversal skills. In our interviews, one expert says: "There is an increasing shift away from individual performance to more an ability to be part of a team, to successfully run a team, maintain a team's morale and [...] build in a company culture, for instance."

Another important point where experts agree is: "New professions will emerge that require far more creativity and flexibility than many of today's professions." Creativity will also be a transversal skill that covers all kinds of jobs. Flexibility refers not only to flexible working hours but to job flexibility. This kind of flexibility and adaptation to a fast-changing job structure also has an influence on job stability. In future, many job changes in a lifetime will be probable, and more training opportunities for adults will be important in order to keep updating the labor market. Also, demographic change and longevity would indicate the necessity to upgrade and update skills throughout life. However, the Delphi experts in general agree that tomorrow's highly skilled and creative workers will not significantly differ from those of today.

To sum up, training and education will have an important role in the future. Lifelong learning and adult training will allow vulnerable groups to upskill and ensure their access to work. The Delphi experts confirm that education policy will be a decisive issue for local and national authorities (84.91% of agreement). Moreover, an important aspect is that in future the entire system might change; inter- and transdisciplinarity or "thinking out of the box" will become more important, while current academies continue mostly to think in disciplinary boxes. This will be a great challenge for the entire education system, but complex thinking and problem-solving needs complex knowledge across disciplines.

However, there are several risks related to training and upskilling depending on the kind of jobs. Studies (OECD, 2019a; Rathelot & Van Rens, 2017) show that low-skilled workers, self-employed and temporary workers, and workers with a high risk of automation are less likely to invest in trainings and/or have a limited access to it. Policy directions should therefore try to ensure adult training opportunities for all kinds of workers during their career. This primarily requires a change of mindset toward lifelong learning and training, by individuals, firms and education systems. It also requires encouraging employers to invest in training their workers. Educational politics should align the education system to the labor market requirements and needs, and costs of adult training should be co-financed by government, firms and individuals (OECD, 2019a).

The changing structure of work may also be affected by the different generations, cohorts or social generations. These could also help to interpret changing situations in the future of work, providing a helpful framework for theorizing the intersection of changing youth and social transformations. In social sciences, the concept of generations was introduced in 1928 by Karl Mannheim (Mannheim, 2017). In his definition, what characterizes a generation is that those who are part of it have the same collocation in the social and historical context and are exposed to cultural influences of the same type. In order to have a "generation" there must be a generational connection. Like Mannheim, by generation we mean people who are born in the same period who have similar values, attitudes and opinions. Reinhardt and Popp (2018) identify six generations:

1. the war and postwar generation (born before 1952)
2. the baby boomer generation (born between 1952 and 1965)
3. generation X (born between 1966 and 1979)
4. generation Y (or millennials) (born between 1980 and 1995)
5. generation Z (born between 1996 and 2009)
6. generation App (born after 2010)

The authors (Reinhardt & Popp, 2018) describe how each of these generations have a different attitude toward the labor market. The first one is mainly in retirement today. In general, in this generation, men have a continued work biography and women have little employment, are loyal to their employers and do not have a lot of changes in their working life. The baby boomer generation is characterized by a growing economy. Nowadays they are those with the most executive positions, but there will a huge problem to replace them when they go into retirement. They are used to working 40 hours a week and more, increasingly women are employed. Generation X is characterized by a growing individualization. Even though there is a bigger share of (highly) qualified women, they continue to take care of family. Generation Y has grown up with the new media and is the first generation of digital natives, has a strong international orientation and wants a good balance between job, family and leisure. Hurrelmann and Albrecht (2014) define them as the "secret revolutionary," because they will introduce considerable changes in the world of living and working. They are used to having temporary job positions, men and women have similar chances, compatibility between work and family is very important and loyalty and identification with the employer is less (see also Chapter 4.1). Generation Z, born after 1996, has experienced a lot of crisis: from terror to economic, financial and ecological crisis. They grew up in stable families but prefer not to take on too much responsibility. They are generally narcissistic and concentrate on their own individual quality of life. While this may be true for work-related issues, we also consider that this is the generation of the "Fridays for future" and they have a strong sense of society and concern for the future. Generation App will be responsible for big changes in society. They are growing up with smartphones, computers and the internet in general and these technologies are part of their life. They will mainly live in urban areas and their social (virtual) life will have an important impact. Of course, it is not possible to make firm affirmations about the future for all generations, but what is sure is that each generation brings profound changes in society and in the world of work, and that social generations and life phases play a role.

3.3 Conclusion

An important question for the future will be how the meaning and the position of work will change. Work has been the umbilical cord of individuals within society; work gives sense and meaning through social connections and gives people a social position. Work produces collective intelligence and meaning for everyday life and is important for the self-image of individuals. The concept of work has completely changed in recent years. Studies like those of Cedefop, which consider a large spectrum of skills, are important in order to address future policies. Also, the education system needs to recognize that limiting thinking to disciplines will be a problem for the future. Moreover, there is a great focus on perceived shortages in so-called STEM fields (Science, Technology, Engineering, Mathematics). However, little evidence supports the idea of a STEM shortage or, in general, of shortages of high-skilled workers in industrialized countries (Teitelbaum, 2018). The problem seems to be an oversupply of high-skilled jobs and a general pattern of overeducation emphasized because of the Global Talent Competition. This means that policies have to focus on how to ease skilled migration; to ensure better lifelong learning, training and an education system based on evidence-based needs; and to involve and encourage businesses to be involved in training and invest in skills at their disposal.

References

Beaudry, P., Green, D. A., & Sand, B. M. (2016). The Great Reversal in the Demand for Skill and Cognitive Tasks. *Journal of Labor Economics, 34*(S1), 199–247. https://doi.org/10.1086/682347.

Bertoli, S., Brücker, H., Facchini, G., Mayda, A. M., & Peri, G. (2009). The Battle for Brains: How to Attract Talent. CEPR Papers. Retrieved July 10, 2019, from http://www.frdb.org/be/file/_scheda/files/Bruckeretal.pdf.

Brunello, G., & Wruuck, P. (2019). *Skill Shortages and Skill Mismatch in Europe: A Review of the Literature* (IZA Discussion Paper No. 12346). Bonn. Retrieved September 25, 2019, from http://ftp.iza.org/dp12346.pdf.

Burke, R. J., & Ng, E. (2006). The Changing Nature of Work and Organizations: Implications for Human Resource Management. *Human Resource Management Review, 16*(2), 86–94. https://doi.org/10.1016/j.hrmr.2006.03.006.

Cedefop. (2016). *Skills shortage and surplus occupations in Europe.* Briefing notes Nr. 9115. DOI: 10.2801/05116. Retrieved September 25, 2019, from https://www.cedefop.europa.eu/files/9115_en.pdf.

Cedefop (2018). *Insights into skill shortages and skill mismatch: learning from Cedefop's European skills and jobs survey.* Luxembourg: Publications Office. Cedefop reference series; No 106. Retrieved September 7, 2019, http://data.europa.eu/doi/10.2801/645011.

Czaika, M. (2017). "Global Competition for Talent": Eine migrationspolitische Herausforderung [A challenge for migration policy]. In I. Altenburg, F. Faustmann, A. Pfeffer, & T. Skrivanek (Eds.), *Migration und Globalisierung in Zeiten des Umbruchs* (pp. 83–99). Krems: Donau-Universität Krems.

Deloitte LLP. (2015). From brawn to brains: the impact of technology on jobs in the UK, Deloitte LLP, London, retrieved September 15, 2019.

Handel, M. J. (2003). Skills Mismatch in the Labor Market. *Annual Review of Sociology, 29,* 135–165. https://doi.org/10.1146/annurev.soc.29.010202.100030.

Hurrelmann, K., & Albrecht, E. (2014). *Die heimliche Revolutionäre. Wie die Generation Y unsere Welt verändert* [The secret revolutionaries. How Generation Y is changing our world]. Weinheim and Basel: Beltz.

Mannheim, K. (2017). orig. 1928. Das Problem der Generationen [The problem of generations]. *Kölner Zeitschrift Für Soziologie Und Sozialpsychologie.*

McGuinness, S., Pouliakas, K., & Redmond, P. (2018). Skills Mismatch: Concepts, Measurement and Policy Approaches. *Journal of Economic Surveys, 32*(4), 985–1015. https://doi.org/10.1111/joes.12254.

Mehta, A. (2016). Closing in on the Skill Gaps? Retrieved November 12, 2019, from https://qrius.com/29593-2/

Mellander, C., & Florida, R. (2012). *The Rise of Skills: Human Capital, the Creative Class and Regional Development* (No. 226). CESIS Electronic Working Paper Series. Stockholm.

OECD. (2017). *Future of Work and Skills. Organisation for Economic Co-operation and Development* . Working Paper. retrieved August 14, 2019, https://www.oecd.org/els/emp/wcms_556984.pdf.

OECD. (2019a). *OECD Employment Outlook 2019 – The Future of Work. The Future of Work*. Paris: OECD Publishing. https://doi.org/10.1057/9780230274198.

OECD. (2019b). *OECD Skills Strategy 2019: Skills to Shape a Better Future*. Paris: OECD Publishing. https://doi.org/10.1787/9789264313835-en.

Rathelot, R., & Van Rens, T. (2017). Rethinking the Skills Gap. Better Understanding of Skills Mismatch Is Essential to Finding Effective Policy Options. *ZA World of Labor, 391*. https://doi.org/10.15185/izawol.391.

Reinhardt, U., & Popp, R. (2018). *Schöne neue Arbeitswelt? Was kommt, was bleibt, was geht* [Brave new working environment? What comes, what stays, what goes]. Hamburg: Stiftung für Zukunftsfragen. Eine Initiative von British American Tobacco. Retrieved November 19, 2020, from https://www.amazon.de/Schöne-neue-Arbeitswelt-kommt-bleibt/dp/3000584188.

Salvatori, A. (2018). The Anatomy of Job Polarisation in the UK. *Journal for Labour Market Research. 52*(1), 8. https://doi.org/10.1186/s12651-018-0242-z.

Sassen, S. (2005). The Global City: Introducing a Concept. *The Brown Journal of World Affairs, 11*(2), 27–43.

Seils, E. (2018). *Mangel an Fachkräften oder Zahlungsbereitschaft? Eine Analyse von Daten des DIHK* [Lack of skilled workers or willingness to pay? An analysis of data from the DIHK]. Düsseldorf. Retrieved December 2, 2020, from https://www.boeckler.de/pdf/p_wsi_report_41_2018.pdf.

Sutherland, J. (2012). Qualifications Mismatch and Skills Mismatch. *Education and Training, 54*(7), 619–632. https://doi.org/10.1108/00400911211265666.

Teitelbaum, M. S. (2018). High-Skilled Migration Policy Challenges from a US Perspective. In M. Czaika (Ed.), *High-Skilled Migration: Drivers and Policies* (pp. 130–151). Oxford: Oxford University Press. https://doi.org/10.1093/oso/9780198815273.003.0007.

Tortuga. (2019, August 9). Il vero deficit? La fuga di talenti italiani e la scarsità di cervelli stranieri [The real deficit? The Italian talent drain and the shortage of foreign brains]. *Econopoly*. Retrieved October 10, 2019 https://www.econopoly.ilsole24ore.com/2019/08/09/fuga-cervelli/?refresh_ce=1.

Unioncamere. (2019). *Previsioni dei fabbisogni occupazionali e professionali in Italia a medio termine (2019–2023)* [Medium-term forecasts of employment and professional needs in Italy (2019–2023)]. Roma.

Voth, J. (2017). Europe's "Skill Shortage". In D. Frey & B. S. Iselin (Eds.), *Economic Ideas You Should Forget* (pp. 157–158). Cham: Springer International Publishing. https://doi.org/10.1007/978-3-319-47458-8_68.

WEF. (2018). *The Future of Jobs Report 2018*. Geneva: World Economic Forum. https://doi.org/10.1177/1946756712473437.

4

Shaping the Future Organization of Work and Life

Abstract The present chapter outlines the future organization of the work and life of highly skilled workers, covering the importance of a work-life balance, the organization of work and the concept of democratic organization. The central questions pursued in this chapter are why a work-life balance is becoming an increasingly important factor for highly skilled workers, how work is organized in modern-day organizations and how a work-life balance, the flexibility of work and the idea of democratic organizations are related to each other. The results show that a work-life balance and work flexibility are increasingly valued by future talents when evaluating job opportunities. While workplace flexibility can negatively impact the work-life balance, these negative impacts can largely be absorbed in democratically structured organizations. Based on this analysis, we conclude that the topics analyzed in this chapter should be taken into account by companies competing for highly qualified workers.

Keywords Work-life balance • Workplace flexibility • Democratic organization • Highly skilled workers

I. Kofler et al., *The Future of High-Skilled Workers*,
https://doi.org/10.1007/978-3-030-42871-6_4

The following chapter focuses on the organization of the work and life of highly skilled workers. In the global competition for talents, companies must have strategies to retain highly qualified workers. The present chapter highlights three focal topics/key issues that may increase employee loyalty and satisfaction: the importance of a work-life balance, the organization of work and the concept of a democratic organization. The question is what a work-life balance means and why it is becoming an increasingly important factor that organizations should consider when competing for global talents. First, some theories and concepts on work-life balance are reviewed, exploring what can be understood by it and which factors have an effect on it. The chapter continues with some considerations on the organization of work and explores workplace flexibility as well as new types of working relationships and employment. Finally, the topics of work-life balance and the organization of work are linked to the idea of democratic organization. In this context, the reasons a shift in power from employers to employees can be observed will be outlined. Along with secondary data and results derived from the literature analysis, several empirical results from our study are presented.

4.1 The Importance of Work-Life Balance

Work-life balance is becoming an increasingly interesting subject for research. Work and organizational psychologists can contribute to the understanding of the topic, but it requires a wider disciplinary or even interdisciplinary perspective to explain the contemporary interest and importance of the subject. Guest (2002) identifies a set of factors that have brought the issue of work-life balance to the forefront of policy debates. The first set refers to developments at work that might be seen to be causing the problem of a work-life imbalance. Due to advances in information technology, the importance attached to service quality and customer care as well as the need for speed of response, to mention just a few reasons, the pressure of work has intensified. Work begins to dominate life and as a result an imbalance may occur. The second set of factors, defined by the author, is related to life outside work that might be viewed as consequences of a work-life imbalance. The quality of home as well as private and community life is neglected. Due to the growth of evening and weekend work, the time left for family life is decreasing. This reduced participation in activities not related to work also causes an imbalance. The final set of factors refers to the attitudes and values of people at work. There is a general agreement that younger high-skilled workers, especially the generation following the baby boomers, are less willing to bring full commitment to an organization and are more interested in an appropriate work-life balance (Guest, 2002).[1]

Due to the importance of future talents place on it, location factors favoring balance play a crucial role when those workers are choosing where to live. Along with factors such as research infrastructure and resources, quality of school systems, cultural and political attributes and regional reputation, access to leisure activities also ranks as one of the top lifestyle factors influencing the location decision of highly qualified employees (OECD, 2008). This means that personal lifestyle needs have an influence on career decisions. In his theory, Florida (2003) defines the three T's as those factors driving economic growth. The three T's are technology, tolerance and talents. While economists have long argued that technology is the key to economic growth, Florida introduces two more driving factors. Talents refer to human capital as a central resource for growth. He argues that talents, which he calls members of the "creative class," do not cluster where the jobs are; they cluster where there is creativity and an attractive physical environment with high-quality amenities and experiences. These include factors such as health care and education as well as recreation and culture. Central to his writings about the "creative class" is the idea that people will move not only to those countries and places where the most attractive jobs are, but also to those regions where they want to live. According to Florida's studies, lifestyle is frequently prioritized over employment opportunities when people are choosing where to live. Lifestyle factors include proximity to wildlife, nightlife, diversity, community, identity and vibe (Florida, 2004). The prerequisite to benefit from these lifestyle factors is work-life balance.[2]

---

[1] See also Chap. 3.

[2] Chapter 5 will focus more on location factors.

It is necessary to clearly define what we mean by work-life balance in order to discuss it and its consequences on the future organization of work. Although the term is widely used, an agreed definition has proved elusive. Several definitions populate the literature (Kalliath & Brough, 2008). Westman, Brough, and Kalliath (2009) state that it is the perception that work and non-work activities are compatible and promote growth in accordance with an individual's current life priorities. Or vice versa, work-life imbalance refers to stress experienced in one domain of life resulting in stress in the other domain for the same individual. Work-life balance can also be defined as a process of finding personal meaning and satisfaction across multiple roles and aspects of one's life. It is an attempt to balance the demands and expectations of one's career, personal life, interpersonal relationships, partnerships and family. This process can be psychologically, physically and personally stressful and incriminating (Evans, Carney, & Wilkinson, 2013).

When discussing work-life balance in the present study, we refer to the relationship between work and the rest of life. It is an individual's attempt to balance the multiple dimensions of career and work with the multiple dimensions outside work that include partnership, family, other relationships and personal interests. Regardless of which definition is referred to, one aspect is common to all: what may seem like balance to one individual may not do so to another. Even if we can recognize objective indicators influencing the work-life balance, such as working hours or flexible and autonomous work organization, they are evaluated based on subjective social values (Guest, 2002). Thus, the perception and evaluation of work-life balance is always a reflection of cultural attitudes and values. Chandra (2012) analyzed Eastern and Western perspectives on work-life balance and discovered that American and European companies rank higher in work-life balance than Indian companies as they pay a lot more attention to it. Western countries have fewer working hours and more generous parental leave as compared to their counterparts in India. While American multinationals focused on flexible working practices, the focus for Indian companies was on employee welfare programs.

In our study, in qualitative interviews with experts, we discussed the question of how social change and transformation may change the value of work and how highly skilled workers with a millennial generation background value the importance of work and work-life balance. Millennials, also called generation Y (see Chap. 3.2), can be defined by a set of characteristics formed mainly by the world and culture they grew up in. They grew up with technology and rely on it; they highly value flexible schedules, teamwork and a better work-life balance; they are achievement-oriented and look for meaningful work. They expect guidance and frequent feedback from supervisors and it is very common that they stay with a firm for only two or three years before they move on to another position (Kane, 2019). In our interviews with experts, we discovered that millennials do not adopt the baby boomers' work-centric attitude, but work still has a high priority. Millennials, especially the highly qualified, want to make a difference and have ambitions. They want to do something meaningful and prefer working for companies that have embraced sustainable and ethical business practices. They seek new challenges at work, a solid learning curve and they look for an innovative work environment with versatility and flexibility in the workplace.

In relation to the work-life balance, the results of our interviews correspond to those of Chandra's study (2012). The work-life balance is still primarily driven by the specifics of the culture and there are only a few patterns of how work and life reach a balance that may be valid globally. For example, one study found that Australians who move to the USA still try to maintain their work-life balance contrary to the American employees, who yield to the pressure to over-deliver, to work late and to extend their work-hours much more than Australians and Europeans are used to.[3] In the discussion with the interview experts we elicited that millennials or graduates of generation Y are very ambitious and motivated; they want to develop their career quickly, but they attach great importance to an individually designed work-life balance and are therefore less willing to accept extreme working hours. One interview expert pointed out that there is a big change and shift in terms of how people look for employment. "One of the most important factors for the millennials and young professionals is definitely work-life-balance, it seems to be one of the key attracting areas, they want to understand what the company can offer them and how much flexibility they have."[4] In addition, 74.58% of the

[3] Statement by an interviewee.

[4] Statement by an interviewee.

experts participating in our Delphi study agreed on the statement that the significance of income decreases when compared to the value of a good work-life balance.

The results of another question in the Delphi study underline these findings. We asked the Delphi experts to rank several criteria according to the importance they have for highly skilled people when selecting a job. As Fig. 4.1 displays, the findings show that the compatibility of family and career, a criterion that is directly linked to the work-life balance, is ranked in the third position. The interpretation of a good compatibility of work and family life may vary from employee to employee, from culture to culture and may change from time to time. The factor "work flexibility" is ranked in position number two. This criterion is indirectly linked to the work-life balance. Highly skilled people who can organize their work by themselves,

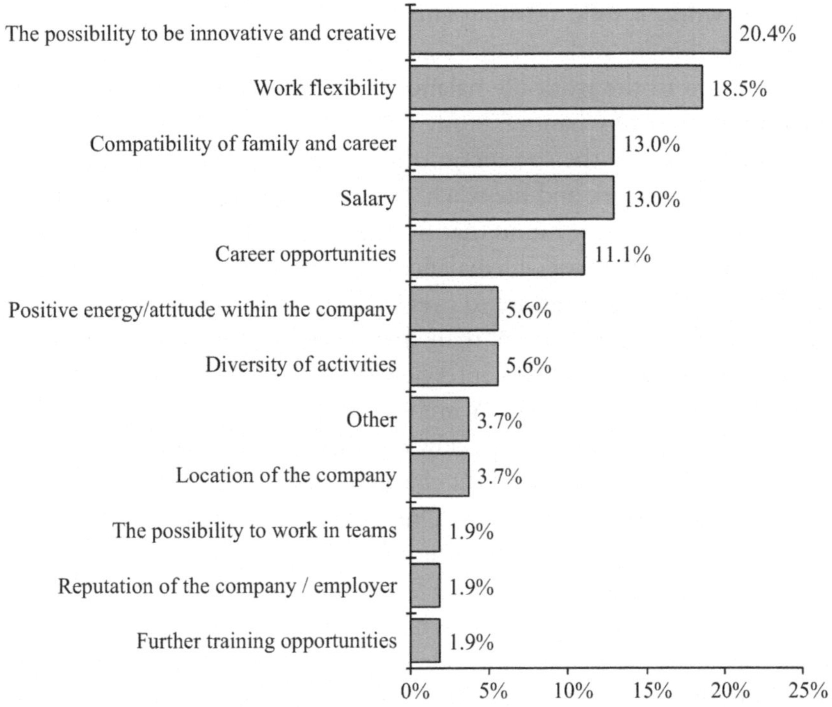

Fig. 4.1 Criteria that influence the selection of a job (own elaboration, multiple responses, in %)

who are not bound to a physical work location and who are flexible in terms of time, can better combine their professional and personal goals.

These results lead us to the next main topic of this chapter. The organization of work—which includes workplace flexibility—is an important issue for employees as well as for employers. Organization of work that is favorable for employees as well as for the company itself can be a motivation strategy and can help improve performance.

4.2 Organization of Work

Today, the organization of work, the type of working relationship and employment diverge from the full-time, permanent and secure jobs that were regarded as the norm in the mid-twentieth century. Many different and contrasting types of work and relationships such as part-time, temporary or self-employment, seasonal working, teleworking and home-working, zero-hours and fixed-term contracts as well as consultancy work are widespread in today's world (Felstead & Jewson, 1999). The full-time, permanent and secure employment by the mass of the workforce was characteristic of the large-scale and highly capitalized economies in the decades following the Second World War. With this organization of work, industrialized societies were able to record an economic upturn and long-range processes of economic growth (ibid.).

For today's highly qualified people these types of work organization are no longer so attractive. What has changed and what will the work organization of the future look like? The patterns vary from country to country, but despite these differences, it can be said that changes are mainly related to global trends and developments and their impact on broader societal contexts. The main developments and drivers of change are described in detail in Chap. 2 of this book. However, some of them will be briefly mentioned here. Demographic trends including aging populations, reduced rates of mortality and declining birth rates as well as the increasing number of single households and changing family patterns have forced female labor force participation.

Next to the demographic change, skill-based technological change influences the future organization of work. The technological transformation and associated digitalization and automation of socio-economic relations change the world of work and create challenges and risks as well as opportunities. It mainly disrupts the concept of workplace and working hours. Additionally, globalization, combined with technological developments, restructures organizations and shatters the unity of the traditional workplace, dispersing work across the globe. Finally, yet importantly, the readjustment of human and social values influences the work organization of the future. This change in values leads to a change in needs and interests, including those referring to the world of work. There is a general shift from work orientation to leisure orientation. This was reflected in the Delphi study, where experts didn't agree that a job and professional position will still be as important in the future in terms of social status.

These economic, social and technological developments are currently contributing to changes in the world of work and, in particular, to changes in the organization of work. They have a direct impact on highly qualified workers. More and more people are working part-time and shorter hours and are engaged in service contracts and temporary work as well as fixed-term contracts. People increasingly switch between employment and self-employment, with an increase in the number of self-employed people (Hostasch, 2000). The results of the Delphi study underline this argument. There was an agreement of 72.01% on the statement that discontinuities in the curriculum vitae are becoming the norm and life-long, secure full-time jobs will hardly exist anymore. They didn't find an agreement that people will no longer spend their entire career with one company. Particularly in the information and communication sector, new forms of employment such as teleworking or home office are widespread. Almost 80% was the agreement that 50% of future jobs will be carried out in virtual offices, service centers, home offices and other smart working forms. There was an agreement of 76.13% on the statement that employees will have to work less in terms of weekly or monthly hours, but they will work longer in terms of years.

This flexibility regarding contracts, the workplace and working hours brings risks and opportunities. Workplace flexibility means that the employer gives more space to the employees and focuses mainly on the work itself rather than when, where and how the employee is doing it. It can be defined as a form of work organization in which the employer gives more freedom to employees to choose the time, location and way in which they work to help align organizational goals with the individual's goals. In this case, employers realize that employees have a private life beyond work as well. It involves providing them with options and alternatives to help them meet the demands of both professional and personal lives (Pahwa, 2019). On the other hand, flexibility may lead to an intensification of work and to a higher level of stress. Flexibility can make it difficult to separate work and private life. There are two types of perceptions workers can experience when relating work flexibility to the work-life balance. They can experience overload, when they have too much to do in a limited time, and they can face conflicting demands from different roles (Foley & Polanyi, 2006). However, with the right type of organization within the company, these negative impacts of workplace flexibility on the work-life balance can also be countered.

4.3 Organizational Democracy

The growth of new forms of work organization and employment contracts has also been linked to parallel developments in organizational structures and labor processes. Like labor markets, organizations are also facing turbulent and changing environments around them and are feeling the enormous impact of globalization on their style of work, leadership and employee management. Increased economic interdependence, globalization as well as the intense competition for highly qualified workers or pressured organizations consider and create human capital as a source of competitive advantage (Ahmend, Adeel, Ali, & Rehmann, 2019). An ethical and efficient way to manage today's technological advanced and complex organizations is to bring democracy into workplace practices (Geçkil & Tikici, 2015).

The design of modern-day organizations is increasingly characterized by horizontal structures and flat hierarchies, by the empowerment of employees as well as by a participatory style of management and decision-making (Yazdani, 2010). Nowadays, it is widely recognized that applying democratic rules and principles within organizations is appealing. Organizational democracy means that employees participate in the processes of organizing and governance and is frequently associated with increased employee involvement and satisfaction, higher levels of innovation, increased stakeholder commitment and thus also with enhanced organizational performance (Harrison & Freeman, 2004). A democratic organization structure is transparent; it has several leaders on different levels and initiatives coming from employees are encouraged. Its aim is a significant degree of worker participation in decision-making and the implementation of mechanisms to allow for delegation and empowerment. Employees are given greater autonomy and they are motivated by meaningful work (Feldberg & Glenn, 1983; Kerr, 2004; Rothschild, 1986).

Principles and common traits of democratic organizations correspond most closely to work flexibility, work-life balance and the expectations of future talents belonging to generation Y. Foley and Polanyi (2006) point out that in democratic organizations employees have greater control over working and overtime hours as well as schedules, thereby benefitting their work-life balance. Employees belonging to generation Y often prefer a democratic structure to traditional top-down and hierarchical models (Chandler, 1962), because they feel that their opinions are wanted and that their efforts are appreciated. The idea that those at the top make plans and decisions and everyone else must follow orders and implement and execute them is not what millennials expect from an attractive workplace. Rather, bottom-up (Mintzberg, 1987) and democratic approaches have proven themselves. Moreover, these approaches place emphasis on the unpredictable nature of an ever-changing environment. This means that, even from a management perspective, including employees in the strategy formulation and implementation processes is not only an important step to attract young skilled people, but it is desirable and inevitable for organizations facing changing environments as well (Markides, 1999).

However, the implementation of bottom-up approaches and democratic organization structures is also associated with a shift in power from the top or management level to employees. It reduces the managers' or employers' power and minimizes the importance of hierarchy in organizations. This shift in power is exacerbated by the shortage of labor. Our study showed that due to the skills shortage and lack of highly qualified people in several European countries, the relationship between employer and employee is changing. One of the interviewees noted that in the future, companies would have to take a much stronger and more proactive approach to the acquisition of highly qualified employees. They will have to go to universities to present themselves as attractive employers.

Companies will have to think about how to attract talents. Here, the shift in power from the employer to the employee can be observed.

As previously mentioned, democratic structures in organizations bring several advantages. Ahmend et al. (2019) stated that bringing democratization to the workplace enhances employee commitment and reduces the intention to leave the organization. However, alongside these advantages, disadvantages should also be considered. Democratic processes can absorb significant time and other organizational resources and slow down decision-making processes, which may lead to reduced efficiency (Harrison & Freeman, 2004). They may carry risks related to the assumption of the responsibility for failure and bad ideas as well as a knowledge deficit, because there is no guarantee that employees have the necessary experience to provide feedback and make the right decision. Implementing democratic principles and processes requires a careful study of both the organization-specific circumstances and its employees to develop case-by-case solutions (Poole, 1986; Sattelberger, Welpe, & Boes, 2015).

Nevertheless, the implementation of democratic processes in organizations may be a promising measure to counteract the acute shortage of skilled workers in the future, as it reduces the intention of employees to leave the organization. Moreover, practical case studies suggest that, if implemented successfully, democratic organizations can be very successful not only economically but socially. Democratization in the workplace and democratic organizations can enhance citizenship behavior and can have a positive impact on society's understanding of democracy (Ahmend et al., 2019; Borsch & Borsch, 2019). Herzog (2019) emphasizes that democratic participation must be practiced in everyday life. If people only experience hierarchical structures in their work, where they spend a large part of their time, how can they then acquire the capacity for democratic participation and an understanding of what democracy means. A similar statement is made by Borsch & Borsch (2019), who argue that we can hardly call our society democratic as long as important organizations such as the public administration, companies, associations and parties within them are managed like oligarchies (Borsch & Borsch, 2019, p. 13).

References

Ahmend, K., Adeel, A., Ali, R., & Rehmann, R. U. (2019). Organizational Democracy and Employee Outcomes: The Mediating Role of Organizational Justice. *Business Strategy and Development, 2*(3), 204–219.

Borsch, H., & Borsch, D. (2019). *Demokratisierung in der Organisation: Das Verantwortungsprinzip und das Grundrecht der freien Entfaltung der Persönlichkeit* [Democratization in the organisation: the principle of responsibility and the fundamental right to free development of the personality]. Stuttgart: Schäffer-Poeschel.

Chandler, A. (1962). *Strategy and Structure: Chapters in the History of Industrial Enterprise*. New York: Doubleday.

Chandra, V. (2012). Work Life Balance: Eastern and Western Perspectives. *The International Journal of Human Resource Management, 23*(5), 1040–1056.

Evans, A. M., Carney, J. S., & Wilkinson, M. (2013). Work Life Balance For Men: Counseling Implications. *Journal of Counseling & Development, 91*(4), 436–441.

Feldberg, R. L., & Glenn, E. N. (1983). Incipient Workplace Democracy Among United States Clerical Workers. *Economic and Industrial Democracy, 4*(1), 47–67. https://doi.org/10.1177/0143831X8300400104.

Felstead, A., & Jewson, N. (1999). Flexible Labour and Non-Standard Employment: An Agenda of Issues. In A. A. Felstead & N. Jewson (Eds.), *Global Trends in Flexible Labour. Critical Perspectives on Work and Organisations* (pp. 1–20). London: Palgrave.

Florida, R. (2003). *The Rise of the Creative Class: And How It's Transforming Work, Leisure, Community, and Everyday Life*. New York: Basic Books.

Florida, R. (2004). *Cities and the Creative Class*. London: Routledge.

Foley, J. R., & Polanyi, M. (2006). Workplace Democracy: Why Bother? *Economic and Industrial Democracy, 27*(1), 173–191. https://doi.org/10.1177/0143831X06060595.

Geçkil, T., & Tikici, M. (2015). A Study on Developing the Organizational Democracy Scale. *Amme Idaresi Dergisi, 48*(4), 41–78.

Guest, D. E. (2002). Perspectives on the Study of Work-Life Balance. *Social Science Information, 41*(2), 255–279. https://doi.org/10.1177/0539018402041002005.

Harrison, S. J., & Freeman, E. (2004). Special Topic: Democracy In and Around Organizations. *Academy of Management Executive, 18*, 49–53.

Herzog, L. (2019). *Die Rettung der Arbeit. Ein politischer Aufruf* [Saving the job. A political appeal]. München: Hanser Berlin.
Hostasch, L. (2000). *Foreword. Magazine 2 – The Changing World of Work*. Bilbao.
Kalliath, T., & Brough, P. (2008). Work-Life Balance: A Review of the Meaning of the Balance Construct. *Journal of Management & Organization, 14*(3), 323–327. https://doi.org/10.5172/jmo.837.14.3.323.
Kane, S. (2019, May 28). The Common Characteristics of Millennial Professionals. Retrieved December 5, 2019 from Balance Careers website: https://www.thebalancecareers.com/common-characteristics-of-generation-y-professionals-2164683.
Kerr, J. L. (2004). The Limits of Organizational Democracy. *Academy of Management Executive, 18*(3), 81–95. https://doi.org/10.5465/AME.2004.14776172.
Markides, C. (1999). Dynamic View of Strategy. *IEEE Engineering Management Review*. https://doi.org/10.4135/9781452229805.n230.
Mintzberg, H. (1987). The Strategy Concept I: Five Ps for Strategy. *California Management Review, 30*(1), 11–24. https://doi.org/10.2307/41165263 .
OECD. (2008). *The Global Competition for Talent: Mobility of the Highly Skilled*. Paris: OECD Publishing.
Pahwa, A. (2019, September 5). Workplace Flexibility. What Is It & Why Is It Important? Retrieved November 12, 2019, from https://www.feedough.com/work-flexibility-important/.
Poole, M. (1986). *Towards a New Industrial Democracy: Workers' Participation in Industry*. London: Routledge.
Rothschild, J. (1986). *The Cooperative Workplace: Potentials and Dilemmas of Organizational Democracy and Participation* (3rd ed.). Cambridge: Cambridge University Press.
Sattelberger, T., Welpe, I., & Boes, A. (2015). *Das demokratische Unternehmen. Neue Arbeits- und Führungskulturen im Zeitalter digitaler Wirtschaft* [The democratic enterprise. New work and management cultures in the age of the digital economy]. Freiburg/Munich: Haufe Gruppe.
Westman, M., Brough, P., & Kalliath, T. (2009). Expert Commentary on Work-Life Balance and Crossover of Emotions and Experiences: Theoretical and Practice Advancements. *Journal of Organizational Behavior, 30*(5), 587–595. https://doi.org/10.1002/job.616.
Yazdani, N. (2010). Organizational Democracy and Organization Structure Link: Role of Strategic Leadership & Environmental Uncertainty. *IBA Business Review, 5*(2), 51–74.

flow of finances and information at a global scale, transnational mobility and the division of labor led to the idea of different global processes of spatialization (Günzel, 2010). As a consequence of the progress in telecommunication and transportation systems and increased global interconnectedness, some proclaimed the "death of geography" (Bates, 1996) or "the end of geography or distance" (Bates, 1996; Cairncross, 2002; Friedman, 2005; O'Brien, 1992). For example, Kelly (1999) argued that the economy operates in a space rather than a place, and over time more and more economic transactions will migrate to this new space—therefore being somewhere physically will no longer be necessary. McLuhan and Powers (1992) argued that due to growing interconnectedness the world will become a "global village" that will lead to standardization and homogenization of culture and lifestyles, that is, the "McDonaldization" of society and culture (Junge, 2011). In contrast, other scholars highlight the importance of geographic proximity and place (Han, Tsou, & Clarke, 2018; Kolko, 2000; Morgan, 2004).

Nijkamp (2017) argues that distance and its related costs still matter because of uneven access to digital technologies worldwide and because of the differences between the use and access to those digital technologies. Thus, for example, urban agglomerations possess locational advantages over isolated areas. Richard Florida (2003) revealed that the myth of the death of geography is very easy to deflate: "[…] not only do people remain highly concentrated, the economy itself—the high-tech, knowledge-based, and creative content industries that drive so much of economic growth—continues to concentrate in specific places from Austin and Silicon Valley to New York City and Hollywood, just as the automobile industry once concentrated in Detroit" (p. 4).

Additionally, he claims that according to his empirical research, place and community appear to be essential to economic life and real concentrations of people in real places are crucial factors for the economy. Therefore, the global doesn't exist without the local. Roland Robertson (1998) and others coined the term "glocalization" to describe the complex interaction of the global and the local (Steger, 2018, p. 86), highlighting the fact that social, political and economic processes concentrate in or are always linked to a particular geographical location (place).

5.1 Attracting the Highly Skilled as a (Local) Development Strategy

Our economic system is (predominantly) growth- and profit-oriented and all players seem to be in competition with one another. This competition occurs at all levels: between people, companies, regions and nations. Knowledge and access to networks became the most important sources of wealth and power but also of differences (Castells, 1996). Therefore, a central strategy for nations and/or regions to create or secure their wealth and power was and still is to attract companies and industries in order to enhance innovation and knowledge production and to be at the forefront of our globalized and knowledge-driven economy. The technological and innovative capability of firms may bring benefits for the economy and society through the global competitiveness of a country, a city or a region (Venturini, Kalantaryan, & Fassio, 2018).

In recent centuries, the attraction and retainment of the highly skilled or "talents" became an important tool to stimulate economic development and a central part of innovation strategies at all scales and all over the world. One basic assumption is that having a large number of highly skilled or talents within a region support knowledge creation and have a positive impact on the economic development and the competitiveness of that place, even though some experts in our Delphi survey underlined the increasing globalization at the highest levels of talent competition.

It is also an illusion to say that the internet merges places and work processes and that highly skilled people will be able to carry on their activities in the future regardless of where they work. The Delphi experts agreed at 73.09% that location will continue to be decisive, for both companies and the highly skilled workforce. But "in a company working in an expanding sector, employees have more decision-making power in bargaining for their living conditions" (comment of a Delphi expert). These results refer partially to the shift of power to the employees, as people with various skills and knowledge can choose where they want to go (see Chap. 4). This means that skilled workers enjoy greater freedom of movement than others and are more internationally mobile (Czaika, 2018). This division along with educational levels, occupational profiles or diverse competencies led to an increasing segmentation of the labor market.

Kelly (2012) highlights the “elite” character, as skilled or “brain” workers have the privilege to choose where and when to move and have more destination options and fewer entry barriers than less-qualified people (see also Chap. 2). The majority of employees, especially those with low qualifications, do not have that advantage, although those employees are also needed by the economy. Moretti’s study (2013) shows, for example, that five more low-qualified jobs are needed or created for each highly qualified person in the USA; they complete each other. As one of the Delphi experts stated, “we still need people to prepare sushi for highly skilled workers.” Consequently, the economy needs high- and low-skilled personnel, from taxi drivers to scientists.

However, this aspect is not reflected at the national (and regional) policy level (as shown in Chap. 3). The main focus is on the highly qualified, as the trend in migration policy observed in the twenty-first century confirms. National (and supranational) immigration policies show a steady increase of high-skilled migration policies aiming to attract skills and knowledge from abroad, not just to overcome potential skills shortages (Czaika, 2018). Our Delphi results confirm this policy trend. The Delphi experts agreed that more nations will adapt their migration policies according to the needs of the labor market (consensus of 74.2%), but an expert in human resources underlined that “sometimes political reasons will overpower economic realities.” However, political measures and the recruitment of highly qualified and creative people will become increasingly important in the future (consensus of 79.98%). These future assessments illustrate that global talent mobility is strongly affected by the regulatory frameworks of the nation-states and movements across international borders (Ewers & Dicce, 2018). Nonetheless, the experts reached a high consensus regarding the positive effects of talent mobility: in the long term, it will promote relations between emigration and immigration states (experts’ agreement of 77.06%).

The findings show that knowledge embodied in people will continue to be an important economic factor for a growing number of countries, but also for cities and regions. This will lead to further efforts by nations and locations to move up the ladder to become the most attractive or the best place for "talents" and confirms that despite the growing interconnectedness of the world due to globalization processes, place still matters.

5.2 Forces of Attraction for the Highly Skilled

The role of centrality and, therefore, of (larger) urban areas for society and economy has been widely discussed in the literature (Christaller, 1980; Sassen, 2001). Worldwide, cities as economic centers have gained more and more importance and are often also seen as centers for innovation and entrepreneurship, as important drivers of economic growth or enablers of innovation (Florida, 2003; Florida, Adler, & Mellander, 2017). One central argument for the innovation advantage of cities is not just their centrality; it is the physical proximity of different actors that facilitates knowledge transfers and innovation (Storper & Venables, 2004). Furthermore, innovation itself appears to be generally concentrated in larger city regions (Rodríguez-Pose & Wilkie, 2016), an observation that is reflected in the ongoing urbanization trends (UN, 2019). Not only are more and more people living in urban areas, but cities also have a larger share of skilled or more educated people (Glaeser & Saiz, 2004). The Delphi results confirm this trend: tomorrow's talents will live in urban spaces (experts' agreement of 78.18%). If this development is true, what are the reasons for it?

According to Florida (2003) the so-called creative class (see also Chap. 4) is attracted to a region characterized by technology, talent and tolerance and, therefore, some cities have a competitive advantage because of a higher share of highly qualified people and a higher level of tolerance and diversity. Furthermore, technological knowledge should be in place so that growth and innovation can be generated. Krätke (2010) refers to important points of Florida's theory, which should be considered critically, such as his use of the "class" construct and his definition of "creative" people, since everyone has the potential to be creative. Finally, cities are characterized by diversity, but focusing only on highly qualified or high-income groups in the population may have negative impacts, for example, gentrification. Despite the critique, Florida's theory points to an important aspect regarding the attraction and retainment of (highly skilled) labor: the qualities of place. Amenities vary along the urban scale between different locations, and their valuations vary for skilled and unskilled workers. Most research is focused on urban amenities, because cities are generally more successful in attracting the highly skilled. The reasons for that often include, for example, a more diversified labor market supply, attractive jobs, higher wages or a higher purchasing power (Glaeser & Maré, 2001; Moretti, 2013; Roback, 1982). Those aspects are not only limited to highly qualified people but concern everybody.

An attractive economic environment is and will be a prerequisite to attract and retain highly skilled or more educated people, but social and cultural aspects along with the possibilities to learn from others should not be underestimated (De Blasio, 2005; Kämpf, 2010). According to our Delphi experts, the most important aspects that will play a central role in the selection of a location by the highly skilled are accessibility and connectivity (experts' agreement of 87.04%) as well as cultural offerings such as art and cultural institutions (experts' agreement of 76.13%). Those location factors are often mentioned in connection with cities. As most future talents will live in urban areas, it is important to understand the forces of attraction and amenities related to urban agglomeration. The highly skilled may not simply "follow jobs," as advantages other than wages are also important selection criteria. Cities offer a wide range of public goods, such as transportation, health and schooling services or cultural and leisure activities that are not available elsewhere (De Blasio, 2005). Therefore, (larger) cities may have a competitive advantage and despite a variety of disamenities of urban areas, for example pollution, congestion or crime, the share of more educated people is higher in cities and urbanization proceeds. However, each place or region is different and has various quality characteristics that may be important for those who are employed, but also for potential entrepreneurs and, therefore, for those who hire.

Figure 5.1 shows the Delphi experts' assessment of different location factors,[1] where cultural or environmental factors, such as recreational

[1] Multiple response question of our Delphi survey: "Which location factors will be important for the highly skilled people of tomorrow?" The percentages are calculated by the answers per factor in relation to the total number of responses.

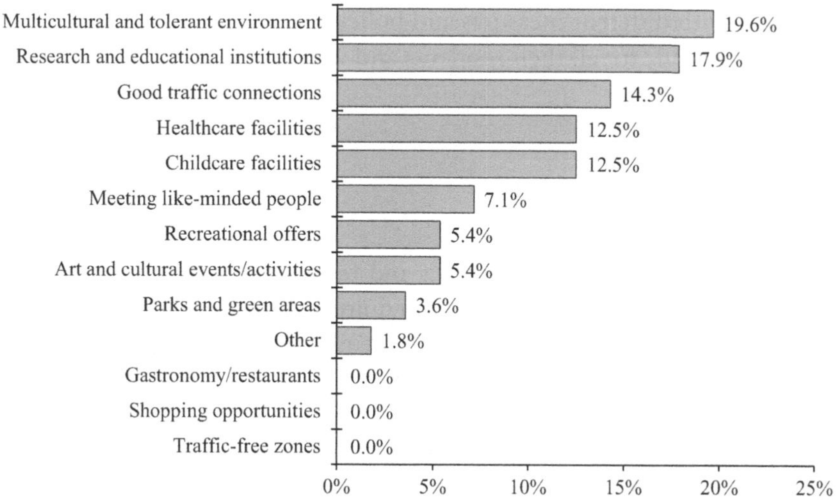

Fig. 5.1 Location factors for the highly skilled (own elaboration, multiple responses, in %)

amenities, art and cultural events or activities, traffic-free zones, or parks and green areas are not the most important considerations. The most attractive locations for highly skilled people are those with a multicultural and tolerant environment (19.6%, experts' consensus of 59.4%). Places with research and educational facilities (17.9%), health care facilities (12.5%), childcare facilities (12.5%), and good traffic connections (14.3%) also have a potential location advantage for the highly skilled, but the experts are divided on these points because some factors depend on individual preferences and life choices.

Although innovation seems to be largely concentrated in cities, it is not just an urban phenomenon (Shearmur, 2012). New evidence shows that many companies and new entrepreneurs are establishing themselves in peripheral regions (Brydges & Hracs, 2019; Rupasingha & Marré, 2018). Despite the results of our study, according to some experts "Sustainability motives will make many want to move out of urbanized centers in the long run" (expert in human resources) or "The highly educated with irregular jobs cannot afford to live in cities" (expert in social sciences). Whether in the city or the periphery, each territory has its strengths and weaknesses, and all have the possibility to improve their situation with different measures and policies, for example, by increasing the quality of life for all their residents and with investments in education or innovation.

5.3 Conclusion

Decisions to invest, develop, attract and retain highly qualified workers are complex and multifaceted and require different instruments. One quantitative instrument to measure multiple dimensions of talent management of nation-states and cities is, for example, the Global Talent Competitiveness Index (GTCI, see Chaps. 2 and 6), a benchmark tool that helps to monitor the position of territory in competition with others at a global level. Quantitative tools such as this index are multi-layered and may expose positive and negative aspects, where each territory has to decide for itself what vision it wants to follow (see Chap. 7). Even though high-skilled labor may be an added advantage for a region or a company by contributing to the innovation process, attracting it also implies policy decisions on factors such as immigration, social equity and education that have multiscale consequences or emotional dimensions (Lanvin, Monteiro, & Bratt, 2019). Even though the highly skilled are more (internationally) mobile than others, they are not the only resource for cities and regions to enhance innovation and knowledge in their territory.

References

Bates, S. (1996). The Death of Geography, the Rise of Anonymity, and the Internet. *American Enterprises, 7*(2), 50–52.

Brydges, T., & Hracs, B. J. (2019). The Locational Choices and Interregional Mobilities of Creative Entrepreneurs Within Canada's Fashion System. *Regional Studies, 53*(4), 517–527. https://doi.org/10.1080/00343404.2018.1478410.

Cairncross, F. (2002). The Death of Distance. *RSA Journal, 149*(5502), 40–42. https://doi.org/10.5860/CHOICE.39-2883.

Castells, M. (1996). *The Rise of the Network Society: Volume I. The Information Age: Economy, Society and Culture*. Oxford: Wiley-Blackwell.

Christaller, W. (1980). *Die zentralen Orte in Süddeutschland* [Central Places in Southern Germany]. (3rd ed.). Darmstadt: Wissenschaftliche Buchgesellschaft.

Czaika, M. (2018). *High-Skilled Migration: Drivers and Policies. High-Skilled Migration: Drivers and Policies*. Oxford: Oxford University Press. https://doi.org/10.1093/oso/9780198815273.001.0001.

De Blasio, G. (2005). *Production or Consumption? Disentangling the Skill-Agglomeration Connection. Version prepared for 45th Congress of the European Regional Science Association ERSA*. Rome: Banca d'Italia.

Ewers, M. C., & Dicce, R. (2018). High-Skilled Migration and the Attractiveness of Cities. In M. Czaika (Ed.), *High-Skilled Migration. Drivers and Policies* (pp. 176–194). Oxford: Oxford University Press.

Florida, R. (2003). *The Rise of the Creative Class: And How It's Transforming Work, Leisure, Community, and Everyday Life*. New York: Basic Books.

Florida, R., Adler, P., & Mellander, C. (2017). The City as Innovation Machine. *Regional Studies, 51*(1), 86–96. https://doi.org/10.1080/00343404.2016.1255324.

Friedman, T. L. (2005). *The World is Flat. A Brief History of the Twenty-first Century*. New York: Farrar, Straus and Giroux.

Glaeser, E. L., & Maré, D. C. (2001). Cities and Skills. *Journal of Labor Economics, 19*(2), 316–342. https://doi.org/10.1086/319563 .

Glaeser, E. L., & Saiz, A. (2004). The Rise of the Skilled City. *Brookings-Wharton Papers on Urban Affairs, 1*, 47–105. https://doi.org/10.1353/urb.2004.0005.

Günzel, S. (2010). *Raum. Ein interdisziplinäres Handbuch* [Space. An Interdisciplinary Handbook]. Stuttgart/Weimar: Verlag JB Metzler.

Han, S. Y., Tsou, M.-H., & Clarke, K. C. (2018). Revisiting the Death of Geography in the Era of Big Data: The Friction of Distance in Cyberspace and Real Space. *International Journal of Digital Earth, 11*(5), 451–469. https://doi.org/10.1080/17538947.2017.1330366.

Junge, M. (2011). Georg Ritzer: Die McDonaldisierung von Gesellschaft und Kultur [Georg Ritzer: The McDonaldization of society and culture]. In S. Moebius & D. Quadflieg (Eds.), *Kultur. Theorien der Gegenwart* (2nd ed., pp. 371–378). Wiesbaden: VS Verlag für Sozialwissenschaften.

Kämpf, R. (2010). Die Rolle der Lebensqualität im Standortwettbewerb [The Role of Quality of Life in Locational Competition]. In H. Pechlaner &

M. Bachinger (Eds.), *Lebensqualität und Standortattraktivität. Kultur, Mobilität und regionale Marken als Erfolgsfaktoren* (pp. 35–50). Berlin: ESV-Verlag.

Kelly, K. (1999). *New Rules for the New Economy: 10 Radical Strategies for a Connected World.* New York: Penguin Books.

Kelly, P. F. (2012). Labor, Movement: Migration, Mobility, and Geographies of Work. In E. S. T. J. Barnes & J. Peck (Eds.), *The Wiley-Blackwell Companion to Economic Geography* (1st ed., pp. 431–443). Chichester: John Wiley & Sons, Ltd. https://doi.org/10.1002/9781118384497.ch27.

Kolko, J. (2000). The Death of Cities? The Death of Distance? Evidence from the Geography of Commercial Internet Usage. In I. Vogelsang & B. M. Compaine (Eds.), *The Internet Upheaval: Raising Questions, Seeking Answers in Communications Policy* (1st ed., 73-97), Cambridge: MIT Press.

Krätke, S. (2010). "Creative Cities" and the Rise of the Dealer Class: A Critique of Richard Florida's Approach to Urban Theory. *International Journal of Urban and Regional Research, 34*(4), 835–853.

Lanvin, B., Monteiro, F., & Bratt, M. (2019). Entrepreneurial Talent for Competitiveness. In B. Lanvin & F. Monteiro (Eds.), *The Global Talent Competitiveness Index 2019* (pp. 3–37). Fontainebleau: INSEAD, the Adecco Group, and Tata.

McLuhan, M., & Powers, B. R. (1992). *The Global Village: Transformations in World Life and Media in the 21st Century.* Oxford: Oxford University Press.

Moretti, E. (2013). *The New Geography of Jobs.* Boston, NY: Mariner Books.

Morgan, K. (2004). The Exaggerated Death of Geography: Learning, Proximity and Territorial Innovation Systems. *Journal of Economic Geography, 4*(1), 3–21. https://doi.org/10.1093/jeg/4.1.3.

Nijkamp, P. (2017). The Death of Distance. In B. S. Frey & D. Iselin (Eds.), *Economic Ideas You Should Forget* (pp. 93–95). Cham: Springer International Publishing. https://doi.org/10.1007/978-3-319-47458-8_40.

O'Brien, R. (1992). *Global Financial Integration: The End of Geography.* London: Pinter for Royal Institute of International Affairs.

Roback, J. (1982). Wages, Rents, and the Quality of Life. *Journal of Political Economy, 90*(6), 1257–1278. https://doi.org/10.1086/261120.

Robertson, R. (1998). Glokalisierung, Homogenität und Heterogenität in Raum und Zeit [Glocalization, Homogeneity, and Heterogeneity in Space and Time]. In U. Beck (Ed.), *Perspektiven der Weltgesellschaft* (pp. 196–220). Frankfurt am Main: Suhrkamp.

Rodríguez-Pose, A., & Wilkie, C. (2016). Understanding and Learning From an Evolving Geography of Innovation. In R. Shearmu, C. Carrincazeaux, & D. Doloreux (Eds.), *Handbook on the Geographies of Innovation* (pp. 63–87). Cheltenham: Edward Elgar Publishing.

Rupasingha, A., & Marré, A. W. (2018). Moving to the Hinterlands: Agglomeration, Search Costs and Urban to Rural Business Migration. *Journal of Economic Geography*, *20*(1), 123–153. https://doi.org/10.1093/jeg/lby057.

Sassen, S. (2001). *The Global City: New York, London, Tokyo* (2nd ed.). Princeton: Princeton University Press.

Shearmur, R. (2012). Are Cities the Font of Innovation? A Critical Review of the Literature on Cities and Innovation. *Cities, 29*, 9–18. https://doi.org/10.1016/j.cities.2012.06.008.

Steger, M. (2018). *Globalization. A Very Short Introduction.* Oxford: Oxford University Press. https://doi.org/10.1093/actrade/9780199662661.001.0001.

Storper, M., & Venables, A. J. (2004). Buzz: Face-to-Face Contact and the Urban Economy. *Journal of Economic Geography, 4*(4), 351–370. https://doi.org/10.1093/jnlecg/lbh027.

UN. (2019). *World Urbanization Prospects. The 2018 Revision.* New York: United Nations.

Venturini, A., Kalantaryan, S., & Fassio, C. (2018). High-Skilled Immigration and Innovation. In M. Czaika (Ed.), *High-Skilled Migration: Drivers and Policies* (pp. 150–175). Oxford: Oxford University Press. https://doi.org/10.1093/oso/9780198815273.003.0008.

PART II

The Future of Work in Europe and Its Regions

6

Talent Competition Within Europe

Abstract In recent times, the ability of a region to attract and retain high-skilled personnel has become an important factor in enhancing its economic benefit and well-being. Therefore, regional benchmarking concerning talent attraction has become a powerful instrument to identify the position of each region in comparison to others and to determine strengths and weaknesses. This chapter presents new findings revealing the strongest European regions in the competition for the highly qualified and aims to gain a better understanding of the regional capability to attract and retain high-skilled workers in the European context. Therefore, every region within the European Union and Schengen was included in our study, as each entity at the sub-national level (be it a city or a region) can be innovative and compete for talents.

Keywords Europe • Talent competition • Highly skilled • Innovation

The competition for talent in the European context is unique as people have the possibility to move and reside freely within the territory of the European Union (EU) with countries such as Norway, Iceland and

I. Kofler et al., *The Future of High-Skilled Workers*,
https://doi.org/10.1007/978-3-030-42871-6_6

European Regions' Talent Competitiveness Index: Some Technical Details

The index includes 15 indicators, subdivided into 5 pillars following an architecture similar to the GCTCI model (Lanvin & Bratt, 2019; Fig. 6.1). The most recent data points were considered in the calculation, with 2009 as the cut-off year. Data were collected in the period between April and May 2019 from different sources at the regional level: Eurostat, the OECD Regional Well-Being database, publicly available rankings such as Times Higher Education World University Ranking, Numbeo, Forbes Global 2000 and national statistical bureaus. Missing values in data were replaced by maximal two-year older data points or with proxies of other territorial levels, such as NUTS-1 or national data. Outliers were detected based on the values of the distribution (Groeneveld & Meeden, 1984), boxplots and normality plots as they may bias the rankings. Data without a normal distribution were adjusted applying a square-root transformation (Cousineau & Chartier, 2010). For variables that still had one to five outliers after the transformation, we applied the Winsorization method (Lanvin, Monteiro, & Bratt, 2019).

To adjust for differences in units of measurement and ranges of variation, all variables were normalized into the [0, 100] range, following the min-max normalization method proposed by Lanvin & Evans (2019). Therefore, higher scores represent a better outcome. Regions were then ranked according to their scores: the highest rank was assigned to the region with the highest (positive) score, meaning that a region ranking first in a variable has the score closest to 100. Each pillar's score was then calculated as the arithmetic average[4] of the variables within that pillar. The final score was calculated as the average of the scores in the five pillars. The average total score represents the basis for the final ranking.

Fig. 6.1 European Regions' Talent Competitiveness Index (ERTCI) structure (own elaboration)

4 Meaning that each variable has the same weight, except for the sub-variables included in the quality of life indicator in Attract pillar: quality of life scores represents the arithmetic average of the scores of the single sub-variables considered. These variables are: (1) life expectancy, (2) share of labor force with at least secondary education, (3) regional air pollution, (4) homicide rate, (5) voter turnout and (6) households with broadband access.

6.1 The Most Attractive Regions in Europe

The overall ranking of the European regions with regard to talent attraction and retainment shows that a large share of the top regions is located in the most innovative countries, such as Switzerland, Norway, Finland and the Netherlands (European Commission, 2019). According to our findings (see Table 6.1), the most attractive region within the European Union is London,[5] UK, followed by Île de France which includes the French capital, and the region "Berkshire, Buckinghamshire and Oxfordshire" in the UK. The best-ranked regions from outside the European Union are the Oslo and Akershus region in Norway and Zurich in Switzerland. The eight countries represented in the top 10 European regions are also part of the top 14 nations at the global level, with Switzerland at the top (GTCI, 2019).

However, the findings also show regional differences in relation to the five dimensions that define the index (Table 6.1 and the box above). Within the Enable dimension, for example, the two regions Île de France and Stockholm have the best scores. The pillar portrays some aspects of the market, business and regulatory landscape within a region, as these factors may fundamentally affect one region's competitiveness, growth, and ultimately their capability for talent attraction. The second dimension (Attract) points to the ability a region has to attract people from both outside the country (e.g. through high-skilled migration) and inside the country. Attraction is possible only when the quality of life within that region is perceived to be high compared to other regions. Quality of life is measured by a series of indicators, covering health conditions, education and civic engagement (OECD, 2019). Other important aspects of this pillar are the GDP per capita and the environmental quality of a region. The leading region in this dimension was Olso and Akershus. But London's position is uncontested regarding the two dimensions Grow and Be Global. Therefore, it seems to provide learning opportunities within an intellectually stimulating environment (presence of top universities or tertiary enrolment rates), to have a high ability to develop global knowledge skills (measured through its tertiary-educated workforce and

[5] Britain's withdrawal from the EU (Brexit) had already been decided, but during the survey period it was still part of the European Union with 28 member states.

Table 6.1 Top ten regions (own elaboration)

Rank	Region (NUTS-2 classification)	Country	Enable	Attract	Grow	Retain	Be global	Total
			Scores					
1	*London*	UK	70.74	79.70	78.25	52.91	94.66	*75.26*
2	*Île de France (Paris)*	France	75.21	70.81	65.88	57.35	79.86	*69.82*
3	*Oslo and Akershus*	Norway	61.82	81.90	51.09	58.60	86.96	*68.07*
4	*Berkshire, Buckinghamshire and Oxfordshire*	UK	61.16	75.27	60.77	52.16	88.78	*67.63*
5	*Stockholm*	Sweden	74.14	78.47	47.51	61.35	72.28	*66.75*
6	*Hovedstaden (Kopenhagen)*	Denmark	67.17	76.06	54.67	62.29	72.90	*66.62*
7	*Zurich*	Switzerland	66.01	78.70	32.76	73.32	74.96	*65.15*
8	*Helsinki-Uusimaa*	Finland	66.18	75.70	46.94	65.43	63.09	*63.47*
9	*Surrey, East and West Sussex*	UK	54.34	70.16	64.53	44.55	82.46	*63.21*
10	*Upper Bavaria (Munich)*	Germany	66.23	70.92	45.36	63.67	62.01	*61.64*

population) and it is accessible at a global level. London's overall score is reduced by its performance in the Retain dimension, where it is positioned at the rank of 101. The leading region in this dimension is Åland in Finland, followed by Zurich and the Lake Geneva Region in Switzerland. Retaining talents seems to require the creation of a safe, friendly and affordable living environment.

As Fig. 6.2 illustrates, the geographical distribution of talent attractivity varies not only between countries, but also within the same country. A deep divide emerges between both Eastern and Western and Northern and Southern Europe. The so-called Blue Banana, the highly urbanized corridor that stretches from the London region to Switzerland, passing through the Benelux region and Bayern, is apparent. Furthermore, the 12 score clusters, ranging from the modest to the leading regions in talent attraction, show a better positioning of urban areas—mostly the capitals, but the map also illustrates strong regions that are not predominantly urban located, for example in Norway, Sweden and Germany.

Even though the position of each region is characterized by the national framework, within-countries variability is also seen in Fig. 6.3: the top positions of the ranking are dominated by urban regions or large metropolitan areas, as previously shown by other indices conducted at the regional level (Annoni, Dijkstra, & Gargano, 2019). As Fig. 6.2 shows, at the national level capital regions rank higher than other regions, except for Germany, Switzerland and Belgium. The countries displaying the highest variability[6] are also some of the largest in Europe: the UK, France (FR), Spain (ES), Greece (EL) and Romania (RO).

Notwithstanding the developments that the labor market is experiencing, location factors still play an important role in attracting a skilled workforce, as we have seen in Chap. 5. This is particularly relevant for rural and peripheral areas, where location factors may hinder people from coming rather than encouraging them. According to our Delphi results, the talents of tomorrow will predominantly live in urban areas (consensus of 78.18%), further accentuating existing disparities between urban and rural regions. However, rural regions are not all the same: they differ in some respects, that is, their accessibility, the quality of their institutions,

[6] At least 30 points of between-regions variability.

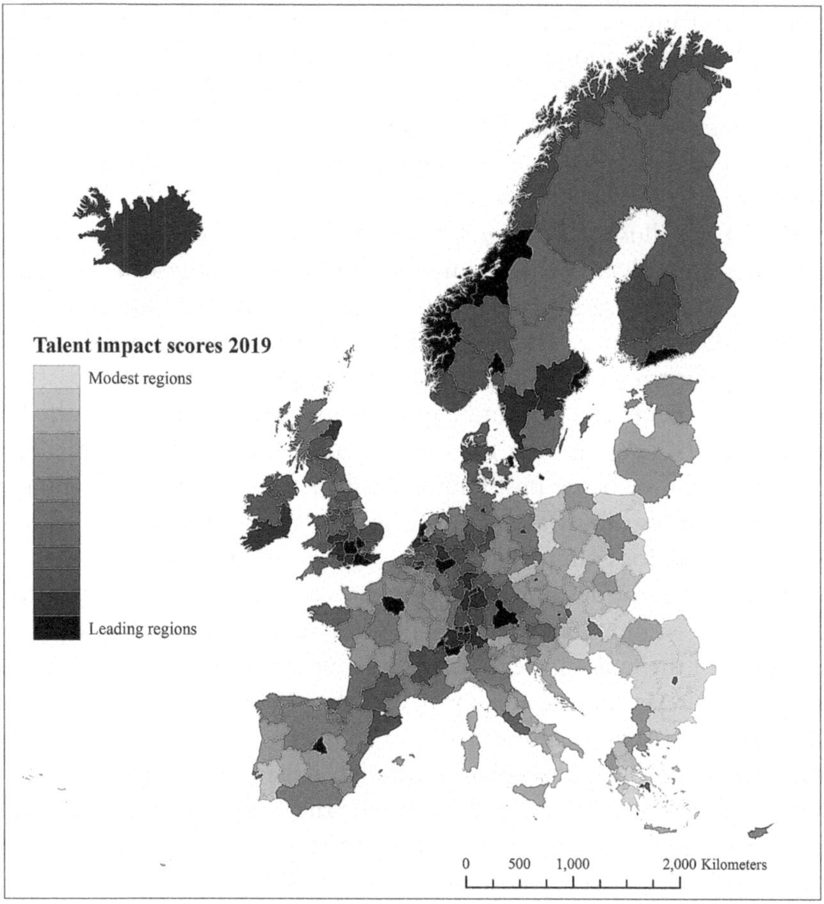

Fig. 6.2 European Regions' Talent Competitiveness Index (ERTCI) scores (own elaboration)

the career opportunities offered and so forth. How could the conditions be created for a rural region to compete on an equal footing with urban regions in attracting a skilled workforce? In order to answer this question, we move our focus in the next chapter from Europe as a whole to South Tyrol, an alpine region located in Northern Italy. The area represents an economically strong region within Europe but is characterized by increased emigration of highly qualified people—a contradiction worth analyzing.

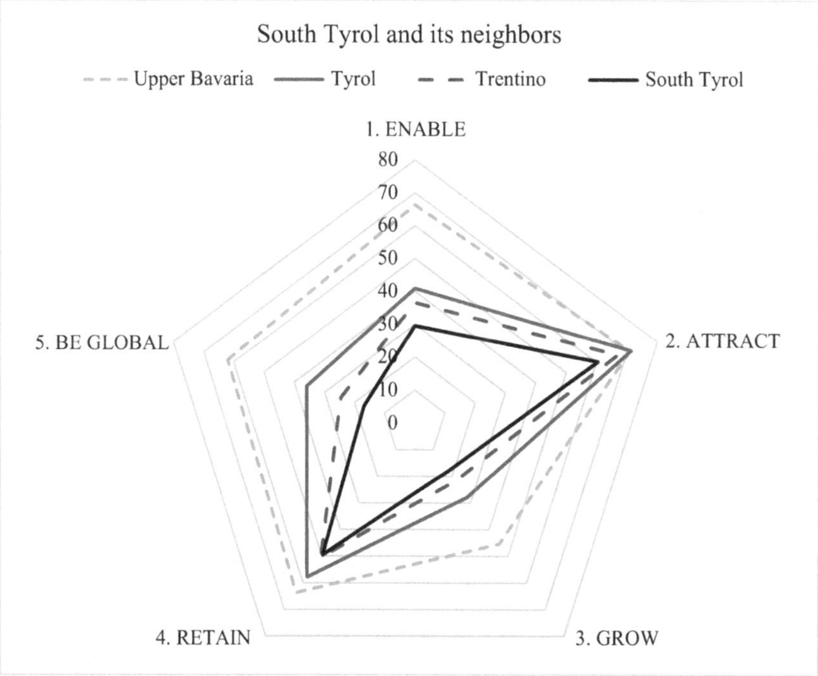

Fig. 7.2 European Regions' Talent Competitiveness Index (ERTCI) scores across the five pillars (own elaboration)

than 250 employees grew by 10 units (ISTAT, 2017). Moreover, a science and technology hub with a focus on innovation called "NOI Techpark" opened in 2017 in Bolzano/Bozen in an area once occupied by an aluminum industry. Here researchers, entrepreneurs and students work together on technological sectors strategic for the region, namely ICT & automation, food, alpine technologies, renewable energies and energy efficiency.

Another indicator within this pillar refers to innovation expenditure. Innovation expenditure amounts to 0.75% of GDP, much lower than the 3% target set by the Europe 2020 strategy and the expenditure in neighboring regions (Trentino 1.8%, Tyrol 3.1%, Upper Bavaria 4.3%). The low innovation level is confirmed by the comparative assessment of regional innovation at the EU level, the "Regional Innovation Scoreboard" developed by the European Commission, where South Tyrol places itself well below the most innovative regions at the European level, despite being classified as a moderate innovator and its innovation performance increasing over time (European Commission, 2019). However, local actors believe the innovation level to be quite high if compared with other Italian regions, especially in the alpine technologies and food sector (Overhage, 2019b). Apart from the recently opened Techpark, the commitment to invest in research and development is evidenced by the presence of research centers in various fields of natural and social sciences (from earth observation to linguistic studies). These considerations suggest that the innovation level within a region cannot be easily measured according to national indicators, as innovation processes need to be analyzed at a lower level (Kofler, Marcher, Anesi, Pechlaner, & Streifeneder, 2018).

The Attract pillar focuses on the two main factors a region can deploy to attract a high-skilled workforce (previously illustrated in Chap. 5): economic performance and life quality. According to traditional theories, migration is viewed merely as an investment decision, where the returns to migration should exceed the costs of moving. Income differences indeed represent one of the key drivers of intra-EU mobility since the highest flows are observed from those countries with relatively low GDP per capita to those with higher income levels and more employment opportunities (Barslund et al., 2014). As illustrated above, South Tyrol boasts one of the highest gross domestic products per capita within Europe, at the same level of German and British regions. However, economic factors are not enough to attract high-skilled workers, as (among other reasons) amenities may also play a role. As defined by the OECD, quality of life refers to human welfare (well-being) measured by social indicators rather than by quantitative measures of income and production. We followed the social indicators selected from OECD Regional Well-Being database, covering the following aspects: health, education, environment, personal safety, civic engagement and accessibility of services. Among the variables encompassed by the quality of life definition, South Tyrol is among the top regions in Europe for health, measured by life expectancy, and safety, measured by (low) homicide rates. This result is confirmed by the OECD Regional Well-being Index, where South Tyrol also performs particularly well in the "jobs" topic (OECD, 2019), and by the ranking of Il Sole 24 Ore, which puts the city of Bolzano/

the German-speaking population (the majority in the region, but a minority at the national level) and leading to a long period of tensions and conflicts. After decades of negotiations on the status of the German minority, thanks to the Second Autonomy Statute, signed in 1972, South Tyrol obtained the level of self-government it enjoys in current times. As a result, rural and peripheral areas were supported from an economic point of view to prevent depopulation and migration, tourism increased, and industrial production took off.

The region is now officially trilingual: according to the 2011 population census, 69.4% of the population speak German, 26.1% speak Italian and 4.5% Ladin, an ancient Romance language. Linguistic groups also play an important role in the labor market: in the public service, jobs have to be fairly divided between the groups according to the so-called Ethnic Proportion ("Ethnischer Proporz" or "Proporzionale etnica") and all public employees must have a language certification. In the private sector, even if the certification is not required, proficiency in German and Italian is highly appreciated.

Notwithstanding economic well-being and a proven resilience to the recent economic and financial crisis, the local labor market is now faced with big challenges such as population aging, migration and skilled work shortages, which have their roots in the mega-trends described in the previous chapters. The share of employees over 50 years old dominates the labor market, while the share of young, high-qualified people going abroad has never been so high at the national level (Oberrauch, Perkmann, & Romagna, 2019; Overhage, 2019a), with the result that, also due to a situation close to full employment, some sectors struggle to find suitable candidates to fill vacancies. These issues have become a matter of concern for local stakeholders and have been widely discussed by the public.

In order to investigate how the region could better position itself in the global competition for a high-skilled workforce, we try to disentangle the implications these mega-trends have for the region by comparing it to the other European regions using the European Regions' Talent Competitiveness Index (ERTCI).

7.1 South Tyrol in Europe and Italy

The following chapter discusses South Tyrol's degree of talent attractivity and its role within Europe by benchmarking it against other European regions using ERTCI. ERTCI was developed following the framework of the Global Cities Talent Competitiveness Index (Lanvin & Evans, 2019) and adapting it to the regional level. As a result, variables refer to five pillars measuring different aspects of talent attraction and retention (for methodological details on the index, see Box 6.1). Our results showed that talent competitiveness differs widely both across and within countries. At the European level, South Tyrol occupies the 216th position on the ERTCI of a total of 282 regions considered, while Italy as a whole is found in the bottom end of the distribution, between Slovakia and Portugal (see Fig. 7.1).

Within Italian regions, Lazio (the capital region) and Lombardy (the region of Milan, historically a highly productive region) dominate the ranking together with other regions in the north and center of the country. Southern regions remain at the bottom of the ranking, mainly because of their inability to attract businesses and high unemployment and emigration rates. At the Italian level, South Tyrol is among the middle-ranking regions as illustrated by Table 7.1, between Aosta Valley and Umbria.

Although a lot of attention is paid to the overall ranking of the ERTCI, these numbers do not provide the entire picture. In order to investigate the determinants of South Tyrol's position at the Italian and EU level, it is necessary to analyze each pillar separately in order to identify the aspects where the region is stronger and those where there is room for improvement.

7.2 Five Pillars of Talent Competitiveness

A comparison with neighboring regions across the five dimensions may help explore the reasons behind the placement of South Tyrol. If we consider its neighbors (Tyrol, Trentino and Upper Bavaria), the situation

Fig. 7.1 Map of Italian regions (own elaboration)

appears to be more homogeneous, with the exception of Upper Bavaria (the region of Munich), which is at the 10th position on the overall ranking.

As Fig. 7.2 shows, South Tyrol performs particularly well in the Attract and Retain pillars, namely those with a focus on quality of life and living conditions. On the contrary, the region appears to be weaker in the Enable, Grow and Be Global pillars, mainly because of low tertiary

Table 7.1 European Regions' Talent Competitiveness Index (ERTCI) scores for Italian regions (own elaboration)

Ranking	NUTS-2 region	NUTS-1 region	ETCI final score
1	Lazio	Center	48.03
2	Lombardy	North-West	45.32
3	Emilia-Romagna	North-East	43.45
4	Tuscany	Center	42.08
5	Trentino	North-East	40.10
6	Piedmont	North-West	39.56
7	Friuli-Venezia Giulia	North-East	39.16
8	Veneto	North-East	38.48
9	Liguria	North-West	37.68
10	Marche	Center	36.74
11	Sardinia	Isles	35.42
12	Aosta Valley	North-West	35.15
13	South Tyrol	North-East	34.88
14	Umbria	Center	34.65
15	Abruzzo	South	34.41
16	Campania	South	33.52
17	Sicily	Isles	32.99
18	Apulia	South	32.78
19	Basilicata	South	30.71
20	Molise	South	30.07
21	Calabria	South	29.06

enrolment rates. Some of the key variables within those pillars will be explored more in detail.

The Enable pillar mainly concerns the business environment within a region, as it includes, among other things, the presence of global companies and innovation expenditure. A low performance within this pillar is mainly due to the fact that the South Tyrolean economy is characterized by small enterprises, in most cases individual enterprises, especially in the agriculture and hospitality sector. As entrepreneurial activity is measured by the number of Forbes' Global Companies within a region, all companies which are not public are excluded from the count. Finding a definition of entrepreneurial activity valid for all European regions is indeed complex, but this point should be further researched in order to put urban and rural regions on an equal footing. In addition, it should be noted that enterprises in some sectors such as manufacturing and services are developing their business models away from the family model: between 2013 and 2017, the number of active enterprises with more

measuring and benchmarking regions, it is also important to look behind the numbers. As mentioned previously, the ERTCI index is based on the Global Cities Talent Competitiveness Index (GCTCI), benchmarking cities at the global level on their ability to attract high-skilled workers. Therefore, it may disadvantage rural areas such as South Tyrol as indicators and dimensions reflect different aspects of how talent is managed at the city level only (Lanvin & Evans, 2019).

Furthermore, each region has its own labor market structure and needs. The first and foremost question that should be asked in a region with the characteristics of South Tyrol is: Does it actually need high-skilled workers? According to Overhage (2019a), the profiles where local companies struggle most to find their employees require secondary education or a vocational school diploma, and are mainly in the hospitality and services sector. Indeed, the local Labor Market Observatory (2019) reports that most of the jobs available in the region are for waiters, chefs and technicians. Thus, the shortage of skilled workforce is a phenomenon that is limited to some sectors and heavily depends on how "skilled" workers are defined (see the Introduction on this point).

Nevertheless, our ERTCI can support the local government in designing policies aimed at attracting talented workers from other regions and retaining local talents by providing it with strategic areas to focus on: not limited to economic well-being for the total population of the region, but also provision of services, proper infrastructure, housing and, not least, good jobs. Innovation plays a central role in the attractiveness of jobs: small enterprises should therefore be encouraged to cooperate with bigger enterprises, but also with research centers and universities, in what has been called a "Regional Innovation System" (Kofler & Marcher, 2018; Kofler et al., 2018). For small enterprises, inter-organizational networks represent a resource-saving and risk-sharing strategy (Kofler & Marcher, 2018). Workers should be offered education and training opportunities in order to acquire the relevant skills to support innovation or to upskill. Moreover, bi- or multilingualism should be turned from an obstacle into an opportunity to attract people from different parts of the world and integrate them into society and into the labor market. Last, fiscal benefits such as those provided by the new Italian legislation on "Brain return" (in Italian "Rientro dei cervelli") to professors, researchers and workers in general would represent an incentive for local people to come back and, hopefully, remain.

References

Alto Adige. (2016, June 13). Referendum aeroporto: vince il no con il 70,7%. Kompatscher: "Prendo atto del risultato, rispetteremo la volontà dei cittadini." [Referendum on the airport: wins no with 70.7%. Kompatscher: "I acknowledge the result, we will respect the will of the citizens."]Retrieved December 10, 2019 from: http://www.altoadige.it/cronaca/bolzano/referendum-aeroporto-vince-il-no-con-il-70-7-kompatscher-prendo-atto-del-risultato-rispetteremo-la-volontà-dei-cittadini-1.102837

ASTAT. (2018). *South Tyrol in figures 2018*. Bolzano/Bozen: Autonomous Province of Bolzano/Bozen, Provincial Statistics Institute.

Barslund, M., Busse, M., Vargas-Silva, C., Kaczmarczyk, P., Baas, T., Peinado, M. I., et al. (2014). Labour Mobility in the EU: Dynamics, Patterns and Policies. *Intereconomics, 49,* 116–158. https://doi.org/10.1007/s10272-014-0495-x.

Casadei, M., & Finizio, M. (2019, March 25). Qualità della vita 2018, Milano vince per la prima volta [Quality of life 2018, Milan wins for the first time]. *Il Sole 24 Ore*. Retrieved December 10, 2019 from: https://www.ilsole24ore.com/art/qualita-vita-2018-milano-vince-la-prima-volta-AEDSdbyG

European Commission. (2019). Regional Innovation Scoreboard 2019. Retrieved December 10, 2019, from: https://ec.europa.eu/growth/industry/innovation/facts-figures/regional_en

ISTAT. (2017). Imprese e addetti [Companies and employees]. Retrieved September 20, 2019 from: http://dati.istat.it/Index.aspx?DataSetCode=DICA_ASIAUE1P

ISTAT. (2018). Indicatori di fecondità [Fertility indicators]. Retrieved September 20, 2019, from: http://dati.istat.it/Index.aspx?DataSetCode=DCIS_FECONDITA1

Kofler, I., & Marcher, A. (2018). Inter-Organizational Networks of Small and Medium-Sized Enterprises (SME) in the Field of Innovation: A Case Study of South Tyrol. *Journal of Small Business and Entrepreneurship, 30*(1), 9–25. https://doi.org/10.1080/08276331.2017.1401202.

Kofler, I., Marcher, A., Anesi, F., Pechlaner, H., & Streifeneder, T. (2018). *Regionale Innovationsnetzwerke stärken. Perspektiven für ein wettbewerbsfähiges*

Südtirol - Rafforzare le reti d'innovazione regionali. Prospettive per un Alto Adige competitivo [Strengthening regional innovation networks. Perspectives for a competitive South Tyrol]. Bolzano/Bozen: Eurac Research. Retrieved from: http://webfolder.eurac.edu/EURAC/Publications/Institutes/mount/regdev/Reg_Innovationsnetzw_WEB.pdf

Labor Market Observatory. (2019). *SCHAUBILDER/DIAGRAMMI. Der Südtiroler Arbeitsmarkt/Il mercato del lavoro in provincia di Bolzano [the labor market in South Tyrol]*. Bolzano/Bozen: Autonomous Province of Bolzano/Bozen, Labor Market Department.

Lanvin, B., & Evans, P. (2019). *The Global Talent Competitiveness Index 2019: Entrepreneurial Talent and Global Competitiveness* (B. Lanvin & F. Monteiro, Eds.). Retrieved from https://gtcistudy.com/about-the-gtci/#

Oberrauch, K., Perkmann, U., & Romagna, F. (2019). *Brain Drain – Brain Gain: quanto è attrattivo il mercato del lavoro altoatesino? [Brain Drain - Brain Gain: how attractive is the South Tyrolean labor market?]* IRE Study 2.19. Chamber of Commerce of Bolzano/Bozen (Ed.).

OECD. (2019). OECD Regional Well-Being. Retrieved December 11, 2019, from: https://www.oecdregionalwellbeing.org/

Overhage, N. (2019a). *Cercasi personale qualificato!? Il punto di vista delle imprese altoatesine [Qualified workers wanted!? The point of view of South Tyrolean companies]*. IRE Report 3.19. Chamber of Commerce of Bolzano/Bozen (Ed.).

Overhage, N. (2019b). *Innovation in Südtirol ist... Die Sicht der Stakeholder [Innovation in South Tyrol is... The stakeholders' point of view]*. IRE Report 1.19. Chamber of Commerce of Bolzano/Bozen (Ed).

8

Discussion and Conclusion

Abstract Throughout this book we explore the impact of current global trends on the future of work and on high-skilled workers in industrialized countries. We investigated how technological progress such as digitization affects not only labor markets but especially the development of skills and the organization of labor; the differences between social generations and the importance of work-life balance perspectives. Moreover, considering a regional benchmarking, we explored talent competitiveness of European regions and identified strengths and weaknesses of our case study from South Tyrol (Italy). In this final chapter, we present further thoughts on the importance of work and dignity in dynamically changing societies in the twenty-first century.

Keywords Future • Work • Dignity

The trick to successfully manage the future of work, at least in part, lies in connecting global and local issues in an intelligent way—which is also the goal of this book. Some gain knowledge and understanding of the

I. Kofler et al., *The Future of High-Skilled Workers*,
https://doi.org/10.1007/978-3-030-42871-6_8

situation by looking at the global challenges, others by considering local problems and challenges. The ideal is to combine both approaches, as this highlights influencing factors and interdependencies, thereby either expanding the range of possibilities or narrowing them until the interconnections clearly show how certain developments at the global level will ultimately affect the local and regional level, or how specific regional aspects can develop based on global conditions.

The relationship between people and technology and how it will develop in the future is a major issue. In early discussions about technology, it was considered that the effect of technology on society would make people freer in a certain sense, giving them more room to maneuver thanks to technical developments. In more recent history, it was probably the development of nuclear technology in particular that helped large groups of people understand that technical developments could be both a blessing and a curse. Few would dispute the benefits of technical development, regardless of the field. Over time, however, the shapes of the connections between technology and society have become much clearer, often revealing negative consequences. This is particularly apparent in the broad discussions surrounding social media and new technologies, and their consequences for social interactions. Ultimately, the question is always which technologies can fulfill which purposes—or, to put it another way, which goals can be associated with technological development as a whole? Is it about creating innovation and improving economic efficiency? About social sustainability? Or about quality and price? Clearly, a lack of awareness about the problems makes it difficult to assess the impact of technical development. The discussions surrounding climate change, for example, increasingly show what happens when technical developments transform the framework conditions for economics, life and work so extensively that we can at least begin to see the limitations of these developments alongside the greater freedoms they offer.

One big question runs through this discussion as a common thread: what technologies can offer the best possible progress with the fewest negative consequences? In other words, what technologies are actually worth developing?

The answer to that depends on the consequences these developments will have for the world of work. Scholars in various disciplines have long debated whether the increasing trend toward automation and mechanization might make work obsolete, or whether it would conversely create more jobs and wealth. This always raises new questions, one that is discussed again and again with reference to the generations that represent potential markets (e.g. Generation Z): how do workers perceive the issue of work, and—given the economic and social framework conditions—to what extent are people willing to give up additional income, for instance, in exchange for free time? As history has shown repeatedly, economic systems achieve success by improving productivity, but at the same time they create a growing segment of unemployed people and workers with poor buying power who are thus unable to purchase the goods. Keynes defined the issue of "technological unemployment," emphasizing that economic systems generally achieve savings and productivity gains more quickly than they are able to find new uses for the redundant workers (Keynes, 1956). Even in the age of Industry 4.0, artificial intelligence and the Internet of Things, one issue remains central: in the future, will there be areas, sectors or industries available to absorb the workers who are no longer needed and/or are freed up in other areas, sectors or industries due to technological development?

Work is an important part of human dignity and self-perception (Rafkin, 2004). It's not just about earning money; it's also related to feeling useful and valuable. Not only are psychical burdens increasing in workplaces due to the digital transformation (e.g. in the banking and insurance sector), but fundamental questions are also being posed about the work itself. In the words of Pope Benedict XVI:

> What is meant by the word 'decent' in regard to work? It means work that expresses the essential dignity of every man and woman in the context of their particular society: work that is freely chosen, effectively associating workers, both men and women, with the development of their community; work that enables the worker to be respected and free from any form of discrimination; work that makes it possible for families to meet their needs and provide schooling for their children, without the children themselves being forced into labour; work that permits the workers to organize themselves freely, and to make their voices heard; work that leaves enough room for rediscovering one's roots at a personal, familial and spiritual level; work that guarantees those who have retired a decent standard of living. (Benedict XVI, 2009).

Thus, work is not simply an economic factor, but is above all an aspect that affects people in a substantial way; the goal is to allow individuals to be enriched through their work and prevent them from becoming impoverished in their humanity. It provides a livelihood, but at the same time creates meaning and is associated with a certain degree of respect. Social issues, in particular issues of solidarity, are addressed not just by churches, but in many ways also by politics and science. "Transitioning from a society based on virtual full employment in the private sector to a society whose structures are not centered around the market requires that we change our worldview" (Rafkin, 2004, p. 189). In the future, the common good will likely become more of a focus, which will play a significant role in assigning work a new status. There will be occupational areas that are more adaptable to information and communication technologies, and which therefore will attract new demand markets and competencies. Nonetheless, this "elite" of high-skilled workers can only exist in future's economic and societal system only if most employable and employment-ready people can preserve their dignity through meaningful work. Community-related and philanthropic work will take on new importance through social innovation.

Also, to be considered are the demographic developments associated with an aging population. Because of the aging trend in developed societies, well-educated young people have more difficulty finding jobs, in part because the number of jobs is barely increasing and is often subject to economic fluctuations. The longer young people wait to join the workforce, the harder it is for them to create a progress-oriented career with interesting job opportunities. Conversely, it is difficult for post-industrial societies to give an aging population with excellent job experience—thanks to their successful careers—a chance to share their experience with the new generation of workers after they enter retirement. In the future, successful societies will find a way to merge the experience of a working generation with the knowledge of the subsequent generation. In this context, high-skilled not only refers to learned and easily communicable knowledge (explicit knowledge), but also, above all, to empirical knowledge (implicit knowledge) as the basis for further developments. Such developments are more sustainable when collective knowledge can be facilitated through community-based collaboration. In addition to the intergenerational challenge inherent in designing future-oriented work, global migration flows are also shaking the foundations of established, post-industrial societies, and require new rules for coexisting at the national and regional level. Beyond labor-related migration, the main challenge lies in integration measures, which can only succeed when working conditions and opportunities are carefully considered. Intercultural competencies of entrepreneurs and human resource responsible can be helpful for attracting high-skilled about the special features of a location. This poses a double challenge for regions: on the one hand creating conditions to encourage high-skilled workers to stay, and on the other attracting them. A detailed understanding of the location-specific strengths, and communicating this, is decisive. Diversity, for instance explicitly considering and supporting women in the work world, will be essential in the future when it comes to creating regions that are also attractive for global labor markets.

The complexity of labor market policies also poses a challenge to regions and can't be understood one-sidedly: labor market policy includes education policy (qualifications and competencies at the intersection of social developments and economic necessity; an emphasis on personal development, social skills and overall lifelong learning), cultural policy (the role of work in societies, or hospitality and welcoming attitudes toward [new] employees), social policy (work and its contribution to social development; work as a way to reduce social and economic inequality), mobility policy (quality of a location's accessibility in the context of international location competitions), recreational policy (options in terms of work-life balance; "work where other people go on vacation"), migration and integration policy (internationalization of regional work environments and company cultures), and innovation and research policy (further developing regional strengths in order to improve diversification in sectors and industries, thereby improving regional resilience).

Given this background, regions and nations are encouraged to focus on their "policy of work," with attention given to the economic system. The globally relevant transformation processes pose a major challenge for all companies. That does not mean lobbying on behalf of companies, rather, it means using an integrated labor policy to strengthen the backbones of established companies by supporting their innovation policies.

Increasingly, this needs to be supplemented by providing targeted support for start-ups and establishing start-up platforms, ideally in the context of creating entrepreneurial ecosystems as an integrated network of research institutions and universities, of companies and a "policy of work" or labor market policy. The merging of digitization and operational value chains is creating data-driven platform and subscription economies. Digital worlds are worlds of connectivity and interaction. Abstract thinking and interdisciplinary action provide an appropriate way to deal with new forms of complexity, which in turn creates a significant challenge for the existing educational system to meet the changing needs. High-skilled workers are extremely important for regional development because having a significant number of high-skilled workers facilitate dynamic knowledge spillover. This further emphasizes how important it is for locations and regions to meet the requirements for the "future of work" because while technologies and high-tech sectors have attractive effects for labor markets, talent also looks for jobs based on the attractiveness of the region. Democratic corporate structures support possibilities for participation, and they drive ways of thinking and acting that are designed to contribute concretely not just to the company's success, but also to the success of society as a whole. Without a doubt, large cities and metropolitan regions have an advantage in the global competition for talent—especially because of their accessibility, urban lifestyles, higher-education offerings and wide range of "innovation offerings." Urban areas with attractive rural surroundings can offer additional benefits in terms of recreation. Rural areas tend to gain points with their high quality of life, excellent recreation offerings and, in most cases, safety. Rural regions are not necessarily at a disadvantage in the international "competition for the future of work" if they are able to effectively adjust for the important factors: accessibility, affordable living, work-life balance, educational opportunities, recreational offerings, developing selected strengths and innovative areas and reconciling career and family. The case study in Part II of this book provides insight into the necessary policies for cities and regions as they attempt to shape the "future of work."

References

Benedict XVI. (2009). Caritas in Veritate. l
http://www.vatican.va/content/benedict-
ben-xvi_enc_20090629_caritas-in-veritat
Keynes, J. M. (1956). *Politik und Wirtschaft. Abhandlungen* [Politics and economics. M
Tübingen: Mohr.
Rafkin, J. (2004). *Das Ende der Arbeit und i 21. Jahrhundert* [The end of work and it
century]. Frankfurt/New York: Campus.

Index[1]

[1] Note: Page numbers followed by 'n' refer to notes.

I. Kofler et al., *The Future of High-Skilled Workers*,
https://doi.org/10.1007/978-3-030-42871-6

The manufacturer's authorised representative in the EU is Springer Nature Customer Service Centre GmbH, Europaplatz 3, 69115 Heidelberg, Germany. If you have any concerns regarding our products, please contact ProductSafety@springernature.com

Printed and bound by CPI Group (UK) Ltd, Croydon, CR0 4YY
30/09/2026
02225608-0002